SMALL TOWN CHINA

Small Town China

Governance, economy, environment and lifestyle
in three zhen

RICHARD KIRKBY, IAN BRADBURY and GUANBAO SHEN
University of Liverpool and Shanghai University

Ashgate

Aldershot • Burlington USA • Singapore • Sydney

Published by
Ashgate Publishing Ltd
Gower House
Croft Road
Aldershot
Hants GU11 3HR
England

Ashgate Publishing Company
131 Main Street
Burlington, VT 05401-5600 USA

Ashgate website: http://www.ashgate.com

British Library Cataloguing in Publication Data
Kirkby, R. J. R.
    Small town China : governance, economy, environment and
    lifestyle in three zhen
    1. Regional planning - China 2. China - Economic policy
    I. Title II. Bradbury, Ian K., 1944- III. Shen, Guanbao
    338.9'51

Library of Congress Control Number: 00-134473

ISBN 0 7546 1016 0

Printed and bound in Great Britain by Bookcraft (Bath) Ltd.

Contents

Preface

The economic transformation of China over the two decades from 1980 was arguably one of the most significant developments of the last century. For the almost three decades of the People's Republic during which Mao Zedong was the supreme ruler, China had been off-limits to western scholarship. Indeed, social scientific enquiry of a form recognisable in the West was almost entirely absent. For the outsider, there were of course the accounts of political tourism. But systematic societal research on China, the preserve principally of North American scholars, had to be conducted at second or third remove. A honeymoon interlude for Western scholars of China followed in the wake of the 1979 normalisation of relations between Beijing and Washington. The intrusion of foreign researchers into the villages soon proved, however, too much for Chinese sensibilities. Thus over the 1980s, the huge growth in Chinese studies in North America, Europe and Australasia was not to be matched by an increase in research access. To this day, the gathering of primary data of any kind in China presents Western academics with considerable problems, and these are of course much accentuated when it comes to the social sciences.

For their Chinese counterparts - a much enlarged cohort - the difficulties in obtaining access to the research subject may be fewer (though the deep sense of localism in rural China does persist as a deterrent to outsiders of any kind). On the other hand, the new - indeed the first - generation of PRC social scientists, lacks any systematic apprenticeship in methodology. The contextualisation of primary data remains problematic too, as the routines of collection and publication of official statistics in economy and society remain inconsistent and opaque. The UK partners in the project that resulted in part in this book were of the view that an essential prerequisite for foreigners intent on carrying out fieldwork in China is a competent and cooperative Chinese partner. The presence even of Chinese social researchers in the rural milieu can present a degree of interference - of data pollution. All our earlier experience told us that direct participation of foreigners in fieldwork survey creates a level of disruption and distortion which is unsupportable. In our case, a further complication was the fact that two out of three of our intended fieldwork sites were officially closed to foreigners, let alone foreign researchers. We were thus pleased to forge close operational links with staff members of Shanghai University's Sociology Department, and relied on their experience and skills in implementing most of the data collection at source. It should be remarked too that in almost every research setting - urban or rural - considerable prior effort has to be invested in confidence building and familiarisation with the local Party and government officials. This again is not a task for which the foreigner is fit, although his appearance on the scene at a suitable juncture far into the project can sometimes be turned to advantage.

Turning now to the locus of our interests: this book is one of the outcomes of a large scale research project orchestrated by its three authors in three small towns in mid-to-late 1990s China. Our sites are all *jianzhi zhen* - that is, towns officially designated as such within the formal hierarchy of urban settlements. By the end of the 20th century, the total number of *zhen* had risen to around 20,000, from a mere couple of thousand in the mid-1970s. The typical *zhen* morphology is a central urban core surrounded by a rural territory with a number of administrative villages and smaller settlements. With the continuous expansion of town cores and the proliferation of non-agricultural enterprise, boundaries with the rural hinterland become less easily distinguished.

Chapter 1 offers an overview of the small town phenomenon: its tenor is much in line with that of the growing literature on China's small towns, most of which focuses upon the macro-economy provided by the off-farm sector, usually known as the township and village enterprise (TVE) sector. We are thus broadly familiar with small town aggregate economic and administrative issues, as well as the formal state regulatory system at this level. Less well documented are the actualities of work, livelihood and beliefs as viewed from the bottom up. It is from this perspective that the present book intends to make a contribution, and as China continues to change, to perhaps offer a modest baseline for further enquiry. The present book is essentially a snapshot of circumstances, conditions and opinions in three Chinese towns. There is nonetheless a distinct perspective to the work. This is borne of the guiding concerns of our overall study in the three *zhen* - that is, the increasing tensions between aspirations for economic betterment and the maintenance of an amenable human and biophysical environment. Here is a terrain which the huge scale of China's rural urbanisation process has rendered of intense significance. What is at stake is the sustaining of environmental quality and resources - including, most seriously, that of cultivable land - for China's future generations. The environment-development research fulcrum is central to the analysis of the copious quantitative data generated by the three town study. Our present ambition is to offer a more narrative account, in the main based on extended interview material.

Selection of our three *zhen* was primarily on the basis of degree of economic advancement within three broad-brush regional divisions of China. We acknowledge the inadequacy of a regionalisation into coastal, inland and western-peripheral China. It was the logistics of our fieldwork which determined both the modest number of sites to be surveyed and the utilisation of the tripartite regionalisation. This latter is of course a surrogate for 'developed', 'intermediate-developed' and 'less developed'. Other factors too played a part in the choice of our towns within these huge regional divisions. One of the present authors (Guanbao Shen), along with other members of the fieldwork team, had in an earlier, unrelated study established positive relationships with the local officialdom. These were to prove invaluable in the accessing of local aggregate data, in introductions to a range of key informants, and in allaying respondents' suspicions when it came to our questionnaire survey. It should also be noted that the gravitational factors of political susceptibility - induced by decades in which only the 'model' could be studied and relayed - led us to three places which within their respective regions were probably more 'advanced'. In the small town context this implies a greater development of the off-farm sector, and axiomatically, higher than average output, and greater per capita incomes, a better educated and resourced local administration, and so on.

Now to our actual study sites: Neiguan *zhen* (in the poor north-western province of Gansu), Yuantan *zhen* (in southern Anhui - in tradition far from affluent despite the province's easterly location), and Shengze *zhen* in coastal Jiangsu. In terms of industrial and agricultural prowess, the contribution of TVEs to provincial output, and per capita consumption Jiangsu is at the apex of the provincial pyramid. Our overall study commenced in 1994, and to date has involved four main rounds of fieldwork; the present book represents an amalgam of the qualitative findings of these rounds. Our endeavour from the outset was to develop our research project as a model of collaboration and best practice within the difficult Chinese research milieu. Our largely bilingual research team was, for example, scrupulous in its routines of tape recording, transcribing and translating all interview material - the archive of which runs to over one million words. The first round of fieldwork was directed at the collection of general background data for each *zhen*, enabling the construction of descriptive socioeconomic, administrative and environmental profiles. This was followed by feedback sessions which formed the basis for the planning of the two major data collection rounds. A two-week training workshop was staged in Shanghai, during which Round Two's lengthy questionnaire was successively refined. This process required translation and back translation of questions, advice from specialists drawn from East China Normal and Fudan Universities and the Sociology Institute of the Shanghai Academy of Social Sciences, and piloting of the draft questionnaire in a small town in Jiangsu. Round Two's questionnaire was in due course administered to 133 respondents in each of the three *zhen*. Sample selection was stratified-random, and was based on the household registers kept by the local police. Fifty or so closed questions were included, plus a number of consequent open questions. In the present study, Round Two data are referred to only in the broadest terms: rigorous statistical analysis and interpretation is under separate publication. Round Three of the survey involved interviews with 20-30 key informants in each of the three sites. The resulting material weaves considerably into the present book, and in places is presented more fully in textual and boxed quotations. These provide an often candid glimpse of the attitudes, preoccupations and frustrations of the movers and shakers in small town China. Round Four of the survey provided an opportunity to check and extend data. Additionally, it was the occasion for the non-Chinese members of the research group to appear more visibly in the three *zhen* without fear of seriously compromising data collection.

Chapter 1 offers a contextual introduction by reviewing the role of the small town in China's overall urbanisation strategies. The following three chapters are devoted in turn to each of our three *zhen*. These chapters share something of a common structure, and all reflect the 'environment versus development' preoccupation of our overall study. It is important to point out that these narrative accounts draw heavily on, and to an extent are defined by, the perspectives of the Chinese members of the research team. Being a collage built from a diverse set of interlocutors, the information presented is not amenable to individual sourcing. Neither is the occasional ambiguity in data subjected to the kind of dissection which might be expected in more conventional field reporting. To this degree, we offer 'art' rather than 'science': our principal object is to bring to life these three atolls in the ocean of the Chinese countryside. A further point of style is that we write mainly in the past tense in order to emphasise the fixate of timing. China's development is volatile and certainly much must have changed in Neiguan, Yuantan and Shengze since our survey. This will be particularly the case in terms of ownership of township and village enterprises, for the 15th Party Congress of late 1997 signalled an almost wholesale decollectivisation for most sectors of the non-agricultural rural economy. Finally, a study of just three of China's tens of thousands of rural settlements inevitably raises questions concerning the legitimacy of extrapolation. We can make no special claims here. While our experience suggests that many of the issues, tensions and transformations facing the people of Neiguan, Yuantan and Shengze are common to those elsewhere, ultimately it is the life of these three places alone which we desire to illuminate.

The protracted and special demands of our larger project required the participation of numbers of experienced personnel, both in China and the UK. Much of the primary data was collected - for the most part in the inhospitable winter months - by Li Ling, Qiu Liping, Qiu Hong, Liu Jian (Department of Sociology, Shanghai University). Li Ling played a vital role in the coordination and monitoring of fieldwork and data records. Qian Wenbao was responsible for a number of liaison visits to the towns prior to the surveys, and was also an invaluable support in the initial preparation of computer readable data for Round Two. Much of the extensive translation schedule was executed by Wan Hong, Ed Shepherd, Li Ling and Qian Wenbao. Giles Brown administered the project office during the early stages. Jamie Kenny was responsible for the initial editing of much of the draft translation material. Throughout the project, Zhu Yandong provided essential logistical support. We would like also to record our gratitude to the key individuals in our three towns who made our fieldwork possible, and of course to all those whose candid insights and responses made our data collection possible. Initial funding for the project came from the UK Economic and Social Research Council. Subsequent financial support was provided by the University of Liverpool and the British Council. We are particularly grateful to the staff of the British Council office in Shanghai for their invaluable assistance, both financial and logistical.

Richard Kirkby, Ian Bradbury, Guanbao Shen

Notes on Units and Abbreviations

1 mu = 0.07 hectares = 0.17 acre

1 jin = 0.5 kilogram = 1.1 pounds

1 yuan = approximately £0.08

PRC - People's Republic of China

TVE - Township and village enterprise

1 The Small Town and Urban Context

The Pattern of China's Small Towns

In the China of the Ming and Qing dynasties, the myriad small towns scattered throughout the countryside played a vital role as centres of both administration and economic exchange. Towns played host to the periodic fairs and festivals which bound the society of rural China; they were in every sense the central places for China's great farming population. Most prominent in the hierarchy of rural settlements were the over 2,000 seats of *xian* (county) government. From these places, law was administered, taxes levied, and the larger scale agricultural processing and service functions were discharged. They, along with the tens of thousands of smaller rural centres were also host to a range of off-farm trades and activities - carpenters, builders, blacksmiths, masons, as well as shops and small mills for grain processing, oil-seed pressing and beancurd making. Such enterprises were an indispensable mainstay of China's field agriculture.

Prior to the Communist Party's assumption of power in 1949, China had endured a century of civil war and foreign invasion which had destablised the rural economy, and undermined the economic and administrative functions of the rural settlement system. The tentacles of the foreign imposed Treaty Port system - that modern hem on the ancient Chinese garment - had further reduced traditional agrarian activities and their small town marketing nodes. The ravages of the first decades of the 20th century, culminating in a decade of brutal Japanese occupation, plunged the rural economy into unparalleled disorder. The tragic lapse of the Great Leap Forward apart, China's rural economy enjoyed relative stability and the nation's huge farming population a low but survivable degree of material security after 1949. This, and the new state monopoly of foreign trade, promised good conditions for the restoration of the fortunes of the 50,000 or so small towns (Luo Maochu, 1988: 24). However, the policies of the People's Republic in its first three, Mao-dominated decades proved inimical to the revival and blossoming of the small town economy,

1

dependent as it was on the petty capitalism of trade and handicrafts. Already by 1957, prior to the formation of the communes and the consolidation of state power in the countryside, the new regime had cut a swathe through the web of small town economic life. When the celebrated social anthropologist Fei Hsiao-Tung (Fei Xiaotong) returned to the Jiangnan village of his pre-war research, he found that traditional small industries and household sidelines were in a state of desuetude (Fei Hsiao-Tung, 1994). As for the cycle of ritual and custom, following the formation of the people's communes in 1958, town fairs, festivals and street entertainment, not to mention collective religious activities, were more or less suppressed. Yet during the Mao era there was at a different level an official espousal of a national urbanisation strategy which favoured smaller over larger settlements. The anti-metropolitan tendency was innately endorsed by the Mao faction. It signified a fear and suspicion of the great cities which reeked still of foreign overlords, and it was in tune with their determination to restrain urban investments which were 'non-productive'- in housing and social infrastructure - to the lowest levels compatible with the targets of an intense industrialisation programme.

On a larger canvas, the objective was to maximise survivability of the new state, encircled as it was perceived to be by a revanchist United States, and after 1960, by a hostile Soviet Union too. 'When the enemy attacks, retreat!': the reflexes of the guerrilla struggles of the Communist Party were now once more invoked (Wei Houkai, 1997: 1). Mao's repeated injunctions on the dispersal of China's industrial infrastructure under the *san xian* (Three Fronts) implanted a vast complex of industrial and research enterprises in the remotest regions of the central south-west, far away from the great urban centres of coastal China. But Mao's grand regional strategy, though it discriminated against already urbanised seaboard China, did not amount to a harnessing of China's rural settlements in any coherent national plan. The lack of any renaissance and positive reformulation of the small town economy for the new era was a clear outcome of the orthodoxies of centralised economic planning which began to take shape from the mid-1950s on. The state's determination to squeeze as much surplus for industrialisation as the countryside could yield required a bureaucratic vice on the rural economy. Thus, for most of the period of the rural collective economy (1958-1984), the state's exclusive right to procure and market agricultural goods was rigidly exercised. The farm product of local tradition, more or less diverse, was squeezed by the Maoist obsession with grain. Household handicrafts and service trades, however pettifogging, were severely restricted in favour of state-dictated collective use of the farm slack season. For the Maoists, the 'restoration of capitalism' in China would come not so much from any untoward cosying to the forces of capital - by definition external - but rather from a feared coalescence of petty trading in China's countryside. 'Cutting off the capitalist tail' was the strident purpose of Party power in the countryside, and 'capitalism' was any activity, tangible or merely ideological, which failed to correspond with the Party's diktat. Official antipathy to the 'tail' could be extreme: in the mid-1970s we witnessed peasants being rounded up by bayonet-wielding militia for a crime no greater than tendering a solitary cabbage for sale on the village street.

Such prohibitions denied to China's small towns their function as points of production and exchange for the range of goods and services required by any agricultural community. Instead, the towns were officially construed as mere administrative, social control, and official storage and distribution points. It is nonetheless the case that for many regions, the rural development policies of the Cultural Revolution (1966-1976) did breathe some new life into the small towns. Efforts to improve rural life chances found expression in new schools and hospitals sited in the administrative centres of the people's communes - these numbering some 53,000 towards the end of the Mao era.

In the early 1970s, the rural industrialisation movement begun in the Great Leap Forward was once more applied, this time more judiciously. The emphasis was direct utility to agricultural production, the national plan aiming to equip every county with cement and fertiliser plants, with off-farm activities at commune level encompassing farm machinery, pesticides, and power generation. The impact of the 'five small industries' programme was mainly seen in the county towns and the richer people's communes. The great majority of small towns remained virtually untouched.

This deficiency was recognised by a policy forum of September 1970. The North China Agriculture Conference of September 1970, convened to promote rapid agricultural mechanisation, also called for significant efforts to develop non-agricultural enterprises in rural areas, both at commune and production brigade levels. Again, off-farm developments at these levels were far more successful in richer regions - that is those in the metropolitan hinterlands of the coastal region. An arch example of the late Cultural Revolution was that of the Huaxi production brigade, which by 1978, derived over three quarters of its total output value from non-cultivating operations, including several industrial workshops (Kirkby, 1982). At the inception of the post-Mao reformation in

1978, those places representing the lowest level of China's formal urban system - the designated towns (*jianzhi zhen*) - numbered some 2,200. Yet in 1961, almost two decades previously, these *zhen* had totalled 4,429. While the rescindment of almost half China's *zhen* was in formal terms a function of the 1963 adjustment in designation criteria (aimed at reducing the state's burden in the supply of grain to the population), it is nonetheless indicative of the low priority accorded to the small settlement sector. This is further indicated by the figures for total population of the *zhen*: in 1961 they encompassed 44 million, while almost two decades later the total had risen merely to 50 million.

Questions of Urbanisation Strategy and Small Towns after 1978

The Emergence of Surplus Rural Labour

From the early 1950s to the early 1980s, China's urban population enjoyed the considerable advantages of state subsidy - providing secure labour based on a clear wage system, food and other supplies, and relatively generous housing and social welfare provision. As for the over 80 per cent of the population who were rural dwellers, administrative measures effectively confined them to a precarious existence in the villages and small towns. It is now widely accepted that the collective system of the people's communes, though it maintained a basic standard of livelihood in most areas and at most times, concealed considerable rural underemployment. With the introduction of the household responsibility system in place of the communes in the 1979-1984 period, it became evident that a large proportion of the rural population was not needed in crop production.

By the early 1980s, policy analysts were estimating that almost one third of the rural workforce (then numbering some 350 million) was basically surplus to requirements. Since that time, China has witnessed an unprecedentedly large migration of its rural population. It is estimated that by the mid-1990s, around 80 million persons had effected a migratory shift, about half this number moving permanently to the small towns and cities (World Bank, 1997: 45). By the late 1990s, however, with the rural population growing and per capita land ratios constantly falling, it was estimated that the surplus rural population still constituted 35-40 per cent of the agricultural workforce. Thus after nearly two decades of increasingly flexible employment and residence measures, the pool of labour surplus to the requirements of crop production numbered between 120 and 140 million persons. Here lies China's most pressing challenge - the largest rural-to-urban transition which any nation has ever faced (World Bank, 1997: 45). As China's Action Plan for Human Settlements 1996-2010 acknowledges '...at the heart (of the urbanisation question) is how to handle surplus labour while appropriately distributing the country's non-agricultural population' (Ministry of Construction, 1996: 18).

Establishment of a National Strategy for Urbanisation

The post-Cultural Revolution government's determination to pursue a small towns policy was first formally expressed in 1978 at the National Conference on Urban Work, and later confirmed at the 1980 National Conference on Urban Planning. The objectives were, simply put:

• strictly control the development of the large cities;
• rationally develop medium-sized cities;
• vigorously promote the development of small cities and towns.

(Zhou Yixing and Yu Ting, 1989)

Subsequently, in 1989, when China published its first comprehensive set of laws on urban planning, the 1978 slogan was incorporated in a modified form, which gave greater emphasis to the role of small cities. In 1996, when the United Nations staged its second great Conference on Human Settlements (HABITAT II), the 20 year-old policy slogan was blithely reaffirmed (Ministry of Construction, 1996: 14). The guiding principle was the relocation of surplus rural labour within a diversified agriculture, and in township industries located in towns and cities in the region.

The long-pressed notion of limiting urban scale and preventing the development of unmanageable super-cities is not one peculiar to China. Wherever planners are supposed to plan, whether it be in postwar Britain's new towns, in the Soviet Union of the 1960s, or in World Bank policy of the 1980s (with its 'small and intermediate settlements' programmes), a 'smallist' policy preference is the order of the day. And when the Chinese government's strategy was laid down in the late 1970s, the incentive was particularly great to restrict urban development and to exclude the great majority of the rural population from a big city existence. After several decades of investment neglect, the physical fabric of China's cities was extremely poor.

The housing crisis was severe, and the larger the city, the worse the situation. While per capita housing living space was still at 1950s levels - that is less than five square metres - in the great cities such as Shanghai it was very much lower. Transportation, utilities and educational and health infrastructure were also operating at their limits. Above all, the central authorities were anxious not to increase what they saw as their major burden of guaranteeing grain supplies to the urban population. With the beginnings of reform of the collective system of agriculture, and the prospect of large numbers of underemployed rural dwellers requiring relocation, it was imperative to affirm an urbanisation strategy which deflected them from the great cities of China.

Advocacy of the Small Towns Urbanisation Strategy

The most visible and eminently argued case in favour of a small town strategy derives, surprisingly, from social scientists with a primary interest in making relevant to present day needs the historic experience of China's small town network. It was the foremost social scientist of the older generation, Fei Xiaotong, who by the early 1980s had become the undisputed champion of China's small towns. Many years before China's liberation, Professor Fei had built an academic reputation as much in the West as in China based on his advocacy of small towns in China's economy and culture. In 1936, he and his sister Fei Dasheng were drawn to their home area on the shores of Lake Tai in Jiangsu province, the one to conduct social research and the other to assist in the rural cooperative development programme of that time. Fei's investigations in Kaixiangong - his archetypical '*Jiangcun*' ('River Village') - became in turn a thesis at the London School of Economics, and a book published in the late 1930s (Fei Hsiao-Tung, 1939). Seven years after the Liberation of 1949, Fei returned to Kaixiangong. In his own words, 'I was very much worried about the situation that sideline production was neglected and rural industry had failed to be restored' (Fei Hsiao-Tung, 1994: 4). Professor Fei pondered over the reason why the lives of the local people had failed to improve, despite a lead of 60 per cent in agricultural production. Such thoughts were, however, dangerous ones, and contributed to Fei Hsiao-Tung's (Fei Xiaotong) impending isolation as a 'bourgeois rightist'. It was not until 1981 that Fei could once again visit Kaixiangong: he was to rejoice in the restoration of family sideline enterprises and the newly formed collective non-agricultural enterprises which were bringing new wealth. In all this, Professor Fei saw the renaissance of traditional rural pursuits in a new era in which China was liberalising its overall economy and engaging as never before with the global system.

Why are the endeavours of one eminent scholar significant to this discussion of China's small town experience? In the early 1980s, Professor Fei and his research team (amongst whom is one of the present authors) produced a series of studies under the Chinese title of '*Small towns, big issues*' (Fei Hsiao-Tung, 1984). In the approved manner, the work was both investigative and prescriptive - that is, it spelt out and advocated policies which would further promote China's small towns strategy. It might be added here that if there is one clear case in which China's incipient social science community has had a direct influence on national policy, here it must surely lie. As Fei saw it, the long-established restrictions on migration remained the crucial bar to take-off in the non-farming enterprise sector. The rigid urban-rural divide of the household registration system stultified city and village economies alike. Fei strongly advocated a new regime whereby villagers should have the opportunity to concentrate their commercial and industrial enterprises in the small towns nearby to them. Consequently, in 1984 the government introduced a new measure to permit migration to small towns, particularly to those other than county towns. The main proviso was that migrants should undertake to maintain responsibility for their own grain supplies (the *zili kouliang* transferees).

Anticipating the coming increase in China's surplus rural population, Professor Fei called for a far more diverse pattern of rural life. The main consideration was that the small towns should become effective 'dams', preventing the flood of migrants to the cities where large numbers of newcomers would be bound to lead to human misery on a large scale. Thus we have Fei Hsiao-Tung's (Fei Xiaotong) now famous formula, *litu bu lixiang* ('leave the land but don't leave the countryside'). The phenomenon of dual employment for China's rural workforce - an individual at the same time being both worker and farmer (*yigong yinong*) was already emerging in the early 1980s, particularly in Jiangsu province.

The Small Towns Strategy: Contrary Voices

The relevance of such grand strategy guidance, and indeed whether or not it has actually influenced outcomes, has aroused considerable debate amongst scholars and policy makers. It is clear that one of the first problems is vagueness: 'control' and 'rationally develop' are obviously value-loaded and relative terms. A further problem arises because of the rigid size categories implicit in the slogan: 'large cities' - those over 500,000 - medium-sized cities (200,000 - 500,000), and small cities (up to 200,000) - these are abstract notions which do not take into account the particularities of place. In the words of Zhou and Li (1989: 85), 'The selection of China's urbanization policy should not be based on the size of cities'. We have seen that the most cogent arguments against the small towns strategy as it emerged in the 1980s turn on economics. In the 1990s, an increasing number of analysts inside and outside China questioned whether the small town strategy in its present form is sustainable from the standpoint of land resources and the agro-ecological environment. These latter issues are central to the investigations in our three Chinese towns. Opposition to the small towns strategy on economic grounds came in a number of forms. Some evoke a supposedly Marxist idea of historical development through stages: at its present condition of development, China is said to be not yet ready for a spatially dispersed economy. The nation is 'still at the primary stage of socialism' and as in the economic and social spheres, inherent in this dictum is the notion of inequality between places, in terms both of urban size and of economic prowess. When the time is ripe, the argument goes, such concentrations will gradually dissolve through a trickle-down process.

There are thus those who on grounds of 'historical inevitability' see urban concentration as an unavoidable stage. There are those too who advocate a course completely at odds with the official line: further development of China's 'extra-large' cities - those with core populations of over one million - is the only rational path (see for example Zhao and Li, 1995: 835). Typically, such analyses rely on statistical correlations suggesting a linkage between urban economic performance and urban scale. Most find it strongly positive, though there are some who maintain that the greatest returns will be from further investment in the more 'manageable' cities in the 200,000 - 500,000 range. These arguments in favour of a less rigid formulation of urbanisation strategy rely on familiar Western concepts of economy of scale and comparative advantage. By the late 1990s there were signs that a new orthodoxy was consequently - and seamlessly - emerging. It was one diametrically opposed to the explicit strategy of two decades. A 'correct' urbanisation strategy newly expounded by the State Development Planning Commission went as follows: 'China's guiding principle of urbanization is to plan and develop super-large and large cities, expand medium-sized cities and improve small cities and towns...' (*China Daily*, 18.10.1999).

This volte-face in official line bears the stamp of economistic thinking: China's urbanisation level is regarded as 'lagging' by world standards, and a correlation is made between the acceleration of urbanisation and the expansion of domestic demand. 'Such an expansion rate calls for shifting 85 million of the rural population into cities within the next five years', proclaims the new line. There is no explanation offered as to the means of employing such huge numbers at a time when the crisis in the state economy means shedding tens of millions from the urban economy.

Urbanisation Outcomes since 1978 - an Overview

Transformation of the Urban System

The question of measurement of China's urbanisation rate is notoriously difficult, mainly because of changing official criteria (Kirkby, 1985). But in broad outline, and according to the reasonably acceptable standards established by the 1990 census, in 1980 the total urban population stood at 135 million, 13.6 per cent of China's total. By the end of 1995, the figure had risen dramatically to 349 million - 28.9 per cent of China's total (Ministry of Construction, 1996: 14). Most of the growth has been accounted for by the sub-municipal rural settlements, especially the designated towns (*jianzhi zhen*). China's officially recognised urban places include designated municipalities (*shi*) and designated towns (*jianzhi zhen*). Since the 1990 census, the precise parts of *shi* and *zhen* populations which can be counted within the urban total have been closely specified according to affiliation to various administrative units (Kirkby, 1994: 135, Fig 8.1). At the sub-municipal level, China's smaller settlements divide into two broad groups - those administered by county (*xian*) governments and those under township governments. The former group are designated towns - *jianzhi zhen* - and include those county seats without municipal status, and other designated towns coming under county control (*xian shu zhen*). The latter, far more numerous group includes the seats of *xiang* government (very often former people's commune headquarters), as well as the large number of places simply referred to as 'rural market towns' (*nongcun jizhen*). The three sites in the present study (Neiguan in Gansu,

Yuantan in Anhui and Shengze in Jiangsu) share the status of designated town.

The 15 years after 1984 have seen a quantum leap in the designation of *zhen*. In 1984, the central government significantly eased the official criteria whereby *zhen* could be established. This coincided with a major adjustment in taxation on enterprises owned at *zhen* level. Prior to January 1984, their income tax was set at the rate of 55 per cent, as opposed to 20 per cent for township (*xiang*) and village-owned enterprises. Thereafter, taxation for all rural enterprises owned by *zhen*, *xiang* and *cun* was equalised at 55 per cent (Lee, 1988: 778-80). It was, above all, this incentive which spurred thousands of small towns to apply for *zhen* status. While at the end of 1983 there were 2,781 *zhen* (only a few hundred more than in 1978), by 1984 year-end the figure had more than doubled, to 6,211. Despite some fluctuation (for example, small reductions in the total *zhen* numbers in 1987 and 1989), by the time of the 1990 census there were 11,937 of these designated towns. By 1995 the sector had expanded remarkably, with a total of almost 17,000 (Kirkby 1994: 131, Table 8.1; Ministry of Construction, 1996: 14). There is no doubt that *zhen* designation brings a greater political and economic influence on the surrounding rural territory. Just as China's municipalities have taken on the role of regional centres under the 'city control counties' (*shi guan xian*) system, so the *zhen* have enlarged their boundaries to incorporate the entire territories of the *xiang* which they usually replace (the *zhen guan cun* or 'town control villages' system), thus allowing greater direct control over human and material resources. All three *zhen* in the present study have considerable rural territory under their jurisdiction.

Other Determinants of Urban Scale

As the October 1999 about-turn in official urbanisation strategy acknowledges (and indeed, celebrates), it is manifestly clear that despite the small towns strategy, it has not merely been the sub-municipal settlements which have grown in physical, economic and population terms. Year-on-year double digit growth of the economy, and the weight of attraction of China's primate cities towards domestic and overseas capital, have ensured a thoroughgoing transformation of all first tier and many lesser ranking cities too. Between 1980 and 1995, the number of cities with core populations of over 500,000 increased from 45 to 75; of these, the 'million' cities went up from 15 to 32 (Ministry of Construction, 1996: 14). The many factors which cause the larger cities to be growth poles cannot be given consideration here. It can be surmised, however, that had there been a completely laissez-faire policy towards the complex issues which surround urban growth, including migration policy, the larger cities would undoubtedly have increased in population far more than has actually occurred. It can also be judged that under such circumstances, the conditions of life for a sizeable proportion of China's urban citizenry would be far inferior to those which now prevail.

While the major cities have grown enormously, this does not mean that the smaller cities and the towns have failed to live up to the role assigned to them in official policy. And indeed, there have been many elements of that policy which have positively encouraged town growth. Two have already been mentioned above: the change in migration rules in 1984 which permitted farming families to move to nearby towns (usually the non-county seats), provided they take responsibility for their own grain supplies (*zili kouliang*), and secondly, the easing of official criteria for town designation. As for the former, research by Ma and Ming Fan (1994: 1625) suggests that its effects are significant within a small radius of the town core. Eighty per cent of *zili kouliang* migrants originated within five kilometres of the *zhen*. Research in Jiangsu province in the mid-1980s showed that more important numerically than those who have actually shifted to town residence, were daily commuters from the surrounding rural villages who account for up to 43 per cent of the daytime population. These people were either self-employed or working in town-run enterprises. In addition to the registered town population (made up of both non-agricultural persons and agricultural persons) there was a significant proportion (over 10 per cent) of the population made up of unregistered migrants (Ma & Ming Fan, 1994: 1625). The latter, the registered *zili kouliang* migrants, and the daily commuting population, are a direct function of the liberalisation of China's rural economic policies following the demise of rigid collectivisation. Official data supplied to the 1997 World Bank Report on China (World Bank, 1997: 46, Box 4.2) shows that in the mid-1990s, the cities of over half-a-million received 23 per cent of all migrants. Though this speaks of high absolute numbers, and represents a considerable increase on the mid-1980s figure of eight per cent, it also demonstrates the resilience of the small town sector in anchoring the rural population to the countryside.

Rural Economic Transformation Off-Farm

Regional growth patterns in a number of south-east Asian nations demonstrate the attraction of rural regions on the fringes of great cities to domestic and international capital - a phenomenon characterised by McGee (1989) as 'desakota'. For its part too, China's reinvigoration and expansion of the small town sector could not have occurred in the absence of the required economic factors. Since 1978, a whole series of policy reforms has influenced small town growth. The primary reforms were those which addressed the organisation of agriculture. The process of decollectivisation and the replacement of the people's communes by contract farming under the various 'household responsibility systems' was matched by a retreat of state organisations from procurement and marketing of farm produce. The state still required households to produce and supply agricultural goods, primarily grain, at stipulated prices. However, quotas were considerably less arduous than in the past. Further, in 1979 and on a number of occasions subsequently, the state has raised procurement prices. The question of an inequitable pricing system between agricultural outputs and industrial inputs remains, as discussed elsewhere (Kirkby, 1998). But in the metropolitan hinterlands at least, encompassing much of the coastal provinces and the Yangzi basin, in general the burden on China's farming communities has been eased. Diversification, specialisation, and household marketing of non-quota produce have been freely permitted in the post-1978 system.

As we have noted, during the two decades of the people's communes, petty trading and service activities were largely outlawed and the state's marketing organs held unchallenged sway. During this period private entrepreneurship on even a derisory scale brought down official wrath. But all this was to change in 1984; the reforming government for the first time since the early 1950s sanctioned almost unrestricted private operation of non-agricultural enterprises. These were meant to be on a small scale, with fewer than five employees. In 1982 there were 1.36 million rural enterprises nationwide, with 31 million employees - 9.2 per cent of the rural workforce. The official count for the end of 1986 showed 15 million enterprises (henceforth referred to in the standard way as 'township and village enterprises' or TVEs) with almost 80 million employees. Ninety percent of the units were privately owned, and these accounted for between one third and one half of all the employees.

The remarkable - indeed miraculous - rise of China's TVEs has been the subject of many detailed investigations, including a major World

Bank study (Byrd and Lin Qingsong, 1990). Some headline figures attest to the enormous scale of growth: between 1978 and 1994 rural enterprises owned collectively at town, township (*xiang*) and village levels:

- increased their share in gross national industrial output from nine per cent to 42 per cent;
- increased their share in gross national social output from 7.2 per cent to 32.2 per cent;
- increased their share of gross rural social output from 24.3 per cent to 66 per cent;
- increased their contribution to total state revenue from four per cent to 22 per cent.

(State Statistical Bureau, 1995 and 1996)

By the mid-1990s (the period of our study) the TVE sector was thought to employ around 125 million - or over one quarter of China's entire rural workforce. Considerable diversity exists in China's off-farm economy, with many regional variations. In the early 1980s, researchers identified at least three different 'models' of growth - the south Jiangsu type (diversified collective enterprises established and run by local government organs), the Wenzhou (Zhejiang) type (characterised by household level enterprises and home-working), and the heavy industry-linked type seen particularly in north-east China's Liaoning province (Tan, 1988). The situation today is far more complex and diffuse; the identification of regional models of rural urbanisation is no longer straightforward, and nor is it relevant. The choice of town study sites in the present research was determined rather by the variation in development of off-farm activities, as defined by the broad regions - the coastal, inland and interior provinces. The rich coastal province of Jiangsu, location of our study site of Shengze, illustrates the most advanced (and atypical) regional development of rural enterprises. Two main factors have determined the high degree of rural industrialisation in Jiangsu - firstly, historically favourable natural conditions for agriculture, and secondly, the existence of a mature network of major cities. A diverse and dense communications system, relying heavily on waterways, is an associated factor. By 1994, agriculture accounted for only 15 per cent of Jiangsu's rural economy. Primary and tertiary industries in the rural sector accounted for 15.3 per cent and 30.1 per cent respectively of the province's totals. Most remarkably, in a province with a well developed urban industrial sector, non-municipal secondary industries accounted for well over half of Jiangsu's total. In Jiangsu's case, the rapid rise of the rural non-farming sector has not been at the expense of agriculture. In the richer parts of the province, such as Suzhou, it is the tendency towards specialisation in larger units which has been key. Amongst the over four million rural citizens of Suzhou, it is not now uncommon to find farms of up to seven hectares, enormous by traditional standards. There is a close association between unit size and farm yield. There is also a close link between rising agricultural surpluses and the ability of local communities to invest in non-agricultural enterprises.

Constraints upon the Small Towns/Rural Industries Strategy

Since 1978, the Chinese state has significantly decreased its role in economic affairs. Central state planning agencies now directly control the variables of production and distribution of just dozens of key commodities. The far greater role for the market, and the privatisation of much of the state sector, was clearly signalled by the 15th Party Congress of September 1997. In the process of increasing hegemony of the market, the factors of scale economy, linkage and technological level would in theory give a strong comparative advantage to enterprises in the larger urban centres. In the early to mid-1980s, the proliferation of small rural production units in sectors in which the subsidised state sector remained prominent caused severe conflicts. For example, in cotton growing areas, the newly established rural-based units would monopolise the local crop and transform it into an inferior product. Larger state mills in the cities, often with the latest technology, would find themselves starved of raw materials. In such circumstances, the central ministries would be inclined to intervene, issuing sectoral injunctions to cease production in TVE plants.

The first phase of rapid growth of the TVE sector, beginning in the mid-1980s, was within the context of a volatile national economy. In the aftermath of the 1988-9 period, when economic instability found expression in political unrest, there were moves afoot by the prevailing conservative forces in the Party leadership to drastically curtail the TVE sector. However, the eventual pragmatic judgment was that any attack on the TVEs would risk enormous social costs as well as structural disequilibria in the economy. Thus, in the 1990s, the re-consolidation of the sector was to proceed. It did so particularly rapidly after Deng Xiaoping's unqualified clarion calls to entrepreneurship associated with his

1993 'southern tour'. The key enhancing factor for the industrial TVEs was horizontal linkage to more advanced urban enterprises, to technological and market chains stretching even beyond China's borders. The tradition of enterprise branch elaboration had roots stretching back to the 1950s. It was strongly advocated for the TVE sector already in the early 1980s, when the case of the city of Weihai, Shandong, was nationally promoted (Kirkby, 1985: Chpt. 6). Horizontal linkage renders rural-based production units far less vulnerable to the cold winds of market competition.

Occasionally, by the late 1990s, with the state owned urban enterprises increasingly unable to sustain levels of output under declining government support, mature rural sub-units were able to attain a position stronger and even superior to that of their urban mother plants. In some cities, laid-off state enterprise workers have sought employment in peripheral collectives, thus reversing the historical relationship between the 'iron rice bowl' of the city and the fragile earthenware vessel of the traditional agrarian life. The TVE sector, though always a fluid arena of start-up, closure, and merger, seemed by the mid-1990s to have reached a plateau of stability. Certainly in the 9th Five Year Plan (1996 - 2000) the sector was judged as fulfilling an essential role in the national economy: without it there could be no possibility of absorbing the bulk of the surplus rural labour force. In fact, the 9th Five Year Plan emphasised a cycle of continuous rationalisation of the rural enterprise sector, and close monitoring of its appetite for rural land.

Despite the enormous achievements in the development of the off-farm sector, its structural sustainability over the long term remains a matter of doubt. We argue elsewhere that crop production and thus agricultural land has been structurally undervalued (Kirkby and Zhao, 1999). Thus the newly proliferating rural enterprises have an unfair economic advantage - a headstart over agriculture. This also encourages inefficiencies, in both production and the use of land. The irruption of a rural surplus workforce - China's most prominent social and economic issue - is greatly increased by the inequities inflicted on agriculture.

It has been observed that more so than for other developing countries, small town production may well be chain-linked to national and even global markets. Amongst other negative factors, this implants in a technically unsophisticated rural environment many production processes which are dangerous to both the workforce and to local agricultural environments. At the same time, the interface between local industrial production and local agricultural systems is not well served. Rural industries aim to look outwards, over the heads of local farming communities. A long-term strategic solution, difficult to implement because it invokes huge questions of relocation and restructuring, is to maintain and develop that part of the rural enterprise sector which is clearly oriented towards agriculture. Simple consumer durables, farming and personal services meeting the demands of local agricultural communities should be retained. Other manufacturing, particularly that serving national and international markets, should be concentrated in larger urban centres where external and scale economies, higher technologies, and managerial skills are superior. Here there is more likely to be effective state regulation in addition. Such ideas imply also a more rationally developed network of small towns, with surplus rural population concentrating in fewer and larger rural settlements.

The impact of an increasingly deregulated national economy, and the penetration of regional and global capital into China's countryside may yet bring about a renewed phase of instability to the industrialising small towns. By the late 1990s, much of the product marketed in the domestic economy was feeling an increasingly chill wind: the consumer durables which account for a good part of production do not have a limitless market, even in China. Indeed, warehouses were glutted with intermittently purchased household durables, much of which derive from the TVE sector. It was estimated in mid-1998 that some 15 per cent of all township enterprises were significantly loss-making.

Rates of growth of the sector as a whole were also slowing, reflecting a tightening of bank credit. Already in late 1995, such impacts were evident in our study site of Shengze, where textile markets were in the doldrums and whose smart hotels, once the haunt of droves of affluent buyers from every province, were begging for guests. The alternative escape route from the land - migration to the cities - was also becoming obstructed. With the crisis of employment of the state owned enterprise sector, major cities were beginning to debar rural migrants from a range of employment previously their natural destination ('Migrants go home', Far Eastern Economic Review, 26 February 1998, p12). And with at least one quarter of the township manufacturing sector's product entering overseas markets, the impacts of the undermining of purchasing power and the competitive pressures due to devaluations in the south-east Asian market after 1998 are, at time of writing, still working their way back to China's myriad townships. For the first time, in the late 1990s, the TVE total labour force showed signs of shrinkage.

The scale of China's contemporary transition from an essentially subsistence agriculture to an urban economy is unprecedented in the history of industrial revolutions. The particular features which make China's current experience so dramatic are the sheer scale of population and territory, combined with the ascendancy of the external capitalist economy to a new spiral of globalisation unimaginable even two decades ago. In the post-1978 period there is clearly close dialectical linkage between China's massive integration within the world economy and the new cycle of global penetration of capitalism's production and marketing. This penetration itself reflects significant technological advances in communications, both physical and electronic. Linking globalisation to environmental deterioration, one recent analyst writes bleakly: 'China now joins other countries in a struggle for world position that places nation and region in a cascade of economic relations at the bottom of which lies the rural environment' (Muldavin, 1998: 291).

Media accounts and official studies of the impacts of rural industrialisation upon the agricultural and living environments are by now almost too numerous to mention. According to no less an authority than Qu Geping, father of China's National Environmental Protection Agency, already by the mid-1980s township industries were responsible for one third of the nation's gas emissions, almost one sixth of the polluted water, and a similar proportion of solid wastes (Qu Geping and Li Jinchang, 1994: 161). The growing problem was accorded considerable attention in the 1994 publication Action Plan for China's Environmental Protection, 1991-2000 AD (NEPA and State Planning Commission, 1994). A major survey of 1996, conducted by NEPA and the State Statistical Bureau and involving two million rural enterprises, chronicled an ever deteriorating state of affairs (see 'Survey to measure rural pollution', *Beijing Review*, 29 April-5 May, 1996, p.5).

Though its degree and scale have diminished considerably over the past two decades, rural poverty is still widespread in parts of the country where terrain and climate are unfavourable. In the pre-reform period, strict migration controls combined with far higher living standards in the urban sector created a psychological environment in which rural people yearned for improvements to their lives. Once the controls of the old regime began to ease, and with an increased awareness of the benefits enjoyed in the newly resurgent urban sector, China's rural population were eager to join the bandwagon of 'getting rich' regardless of the price. In a situation of relatively stagnant agriculture, the means to a new life of affluence was perceived as through the development of local off-farm enterprises. In this, local government officials themselves also had a stake, in terms both of prestige and actual material benefit. The universal opinion in China's countryside was now *wugong bufu* 'without (local) industry there is no affluence' (Ma and Ming Fan, 1994: 1642). Thus for villager and local cadre alike, the trade-off between greater affluence on the one hand, and deterioration in customary lifestyle - including local environments and ecosystems - was likely to be settled very much in favour of the former. It was this key issue which prompted our investigations in three towns in three very different regions of China.

2 Neiguan

Location and History

Neiguan is situated in southern Gansu province, approximately 75 kilometres south-west of the provincial capital, Lanzhou. Lanzhou, located on the Huang He (Yellow River), has since the 1950s become a heavy industrial centre and serves as a key commercial and communications hub for north-western China. Neiguan town straddles the border between Dingxi, Weiyuan, Yuzhong, and Lintao counties and has good road connections to each. The Dinglin highway, between Dingxi county town and Lintao county, passes through the centre of Neiguan. Southwards the road leads to Weiyuan county and Tianshui city. Since 1949, Neiguan has been a cultural and economic centre and the seat of local government. The name of the town has been changed several times, but from 1989 was officially known as Neiguanying town. However it was always called Neiguan by local people.

The site of Neiguan claims a long history. In 1976, A survey conducted by the Bureau of Cultural Relics of Dingxi county discovered a site believed to be about 4000 years old. A collection of artefacts, including stone knives and fragments of clay pots, has been assigned to the Qixia Culture. In the Song period, Neiguan was described as a handsome town surrounded by walls. Only scattered remnants have survived, located at the north-west corner of the present town core. Neiguan became the focus of many legends, including the tale of the 'Buddhist trench and sacred water', a pastoral myth depicting the beauty of the area's green mountains and clear streams. From the time of the Ming dynasty (1368-1644), Neiguan was recorded in the 'Zhengshi' historical annals.

After its establishment in the 31st year of the Hongwu era of the Ming, Neiguan village gradually become a focal point of regional trade. According to the Anding County Annals, written in the Kangxi era of the Qing, Neiguan was a town which abounded in produce with a bustling trade, while the local countryside was given over to crop production and animal husbandry. Neiguan attracted traders from neighbouring provinces, particularly Shanxi and Shaanxi to the south. Locals referred to such people as 'guest traders' and their descendants were still identified in the town. A simmering rivalry between the Han and Muslim communities in the area broke out into open conflict during the Tongzhi era of the Qing. Much of Neiguan was destroyed in the fighting, many residents fled, and the town went into a sharp decline. The influence of the Hui Muslims has subsequently declined: at the time of our visit, Han Chinese comprised almost 99 per cent of the population of Dingxi county. Neiguan town recovered somewhat in the late Qing and Republican periods prior to 1949, becoming a centre for crafts and for food and cloth retailing.

With the founding of the People's Republic in 1949 the town became a political, cultural and economic centre. In accordance with the tenets of the Mao regime, from the mid-1950s private trade was gradually eradicated so that Neiguan became solely dependent on agriculture, with a few state-owned commodity shops catering for local farmers. This sharp reduction in economic activity, combined with a worsening natural environment and the vicissitudes of state agricultural policy, impoverished the town. Local people suffered shortages of food and clothing. During the three year period, 1959-1961, when famine was widespread, conditions sharply deteriorated and Dingxi county became one of the poorest in China.

Physical Environment

Neiguan lies in a flat basin at an altitude of 2,035 metres above sea level in the west of the Loess Plateau, one of four Natural Regions within Warm-temperate Humid and Subhumid China (Zhao Songqiao, 1986).[1] The loess, which is a wind blown (aeolian) material, originated in central Asia during the Quaternary interval (i.e. less than 3 million years ago), and occupies over 0.6 million square kilometres in central and western regions of China. The depth of loess over this extensive area varies considerably, from just a few metres to some 200 metres. A key feature of loess is its unconsolidated nature, which renders it vulnerable to severe erosion, particularly when a vegetative cover is not maintained. The removal of the natural vegetation, described as forest-steppe and steppe, from the Loess Plateau Region, for cultivation, fuel and building materials would have markedly increased the rate of erosion. The Chinese Academy of Sciences, using remotely-sensed data, have calculated that around one-half of the Loess Plateau is subject to serious erosion (Liu Guobin, 1999). The soils over most of the Loess Plateau are designated as calcic cambisols (Zhao Songqiao, 1986). Such soils are at an early stage of development, contain very little humus (around one per cent) and have a calcareous layer typically between 50 and 100 cm depth. Throughout the whole area soils have been subject to modification by human activities, particularly cultivation. Topography on the loess region has been shaped initially by river action. The residual hills have often been extensively terraced for agriculture, although in some areas severe erosion revealed little evidence of former terracing. Around Neiguan the overall impression was of maintained terraces, although there was frequent evidence of severe gully erosion. Four rivers - Liujiaxia, Dingjiaxia, Yangyinxia and Zuli - run through Neiguan before joining the main Nanquan river to the east. However, these rivers are highly seasonal, and for much of the year may contain no water. An underground stream, the Xihe, runs from the Huma mountain range beneath Neiguan and now provides the local population with potable drinking water.

The regional climate can be characterised as dry, with cool summers and cold winters. Data collected in Lanzhou, just 75 kilometres away, provide a reliable guide to conditions in Neiguan. The average July temperature is around 22°C. The coldest month is January when the average temperature is about -7°C. There are between 120 and 160 frost-free days a year. Another feature of the local climate is the high level of insolation ('sunshine intensity'). This is due to a lack of both water vapour and impurities in the atmosphere. Lack of cloud cover also results in considerable loss of radiation at night and therefore large diurnal temperature fluctuations. In terms of precipitation the climate is semi-arid. Mean annual precipitation is around 330 millimetres (approximately 13 inches), although there is considerable year-to-year variation. The lowest recorded value, in 1969, is just 249 millimetres (approximately 10 inches). Most rain falls between April and October (i.e. during the growing season) and August is the wettest month (about 25 per cent of the total). The ratio of precipitation to evaporation is around 1:1.5. Apart from the problem of drought, Neiguan is also liable to hailstorms, flooding and frost, all of which can result in major crop loss.

In the semi-arid conditions of the Neiguan area, plant growth, and hence agricultural yield, are closely correlated with rainfall. The problem of water availability is exacerbated by the intense nature of rainfall events, and the porous nature of loess soil which encourages rapid drainage below the rooting zone of plants. Also, the small amounts of rain falling during the winter months are not effective for crop growth. The lack of water resources in the general area poses a major obstacle to further developments and is a recurrent theme throughout this report.

Neiguan's Appearance

There are 17 villages administratively in Neiguan *zhen* in addition to the town core area which occupied around two square kilometres. The total area of farmland was about 120,000 mu (8000 hectares), of which 40,000 mu were paddy fields. Nearly all the remaining farmland was located on broadly-terraced loess. The per capita amount of farmland was about three mu (0.2 hectares). The layout of the town revealed little evidence of formal planning, although the government offices, hospital and bank were all situated in the centre. The area's largest township enterprise, Nuanquan Company, and the County Second Middle School, were located to the north of the town core area. At the south end of town were large markets for clothing, wood and livestock. There were few buildings of note in Neiguan. The best and highest structure, built of reinforced concrete and boasting a toilet on every floor, belonged to the bank. Aside from being the commercial centre of the town, this building also served as a guest house, complete with canteen and shower room. Other public buildings, including the government compound, schools, and the local hospital were once considered town landmarks but had worn badly with age. A large house with high, blue brick walls and four towers was situated two kilometres to the north of the town. This once served as the local manse. Prior to 1949, we were told, the landlord was a Guomindang official, but later the building was converted into flats. Although badly timeworn, the building still retained much of its old grandeur and was certainly a local landmark.

The section of Dinglin Highway which crossed the town, known as '7-5 Road', was an asphalt strip about 18 metres wide. The road served as Neiguan's main commercial thoroughfare and was lined on both sides with shops and markets. Crossing this highway, in an east-west direction was an unsurfaced lane which leads through residential quarters and past a school. This road, like others in the town became muddy after rain and threw up clouds of dust in the dry season. These two roads formed Neiguan's highway system. Other roads were either very short or led into the surrounding farmland. An open sewer about one kilometre in length ran along '7-5 Road'. Although well built, lack of maintenance meant that it was constantly blocked. The town core was very untidy. Commerce had encroached on to large areas of the '7-5 Road' itself. On county fair days, itinerant vendors blocked the road entirely, turning it into a kind of informal market. The congestion this causes was commented upon by many of our respondents.

During our first visit to Neiguan, we stayed in the small three-storey building which housed the town's agricultural technology station. The ground floor served as both a seed shop and the station office. The top two floors were used for accommodation. The station had tap water and could support the hygienic and social essentials of washing and tea-making.

There was no toilet in the building. Instead, people used the next door neighbour's facility which was extremely basic, comprising an L-shaped, waist-high mud wall by the street. Inside there was simply a layer of loose soil on the floor. The toilet was in fact a private manure gathering facility. Its owners welcomed visitors and passers-by to make a small contribution to the fertility of the local soil. According to the station staff, almost every household in Neiguan had some farm land, at least enough to produce grain for personal use. In recent years, the price of chemical fertilisers had rising considerably so that human and livestock manure, which cost nothing, was as prized as much as it was in the past.

Administration

Administratively, Neiguan is part of Dingxi county, which has the distinction of being officially recognised as among the poorest in the whole country. Dingxi had been designated as a pilot county by the State Council for Political System Reform, and Neiguan was chosen to take a leading role within this scheme. Consequently, Neiguan periodically received visiting provincial and central government officials, and occasional foreign delegations as well. Despite its poverty, Neiguan was considered to be one of Gansu's top ten market towns, which reflected well the general state of economic development in this large province. Apparently, Neiguan was considered a window through which the results of county and provincial level development policies were demonstrated to the outside world. As a result, considerable attention was given to the town's leadership. The cadres working for the town government were regarded as up-and-coming administrators and tended to have better educational qualifications than was normal for the region. The Party secretary, a 40 year-old college graduate, was formerly a deputy office director of the county Party committee. The township head was a 41 year-old graduate, who formerly worked in the county's broadcasting bureau and also served as the deputy secretary of Neiguan's Party committee. One of his deputies was a 38 year-old graduate, and former Party secretary for the Nuanquan Company, Neiguan's main enterprise. Another deputy, aged 28, was formerly the office director of the county's centre for agricultural technology. The third deputy, a 36 year old, was an ex-soldier. The calibre of the town's cadres reflected the importance of Neiguan within the county. Furthermore it suggested that the county leadership wished to exercise close supervision over Neiguan's governance. It seemed that Neiguan was used by Dingxi's Party committee as a testing ground for potential county level administrators. County level officials were also often assigned a posting in Neiguan before being called back to regular duties. It was an unusual arrangement and one which put administrators on their mettle. In the words of one official: 'A job here means that you are either going to rise like a meteor or drop like a stone.'

As is customary, the township head (*zhenzhang*) in Neiguan led the local government but reported to the town's Party committee. Before the political reforms of the late 1970s and early 1980s, the town's administrative power was in the hands of the Party secretary. Having examined this arrangement, an investigation group from Dingxi's prefectural Party committee compiled a critical report arguing for a separation between administration and politics. This was simply a reflection, and implementation, of central policy in the post-Mao era which was to separate the Party from government at all administrative levels. The report maintained that:

> The Party secretary deals personally with every issue and is constantly busy while others are kept idle - three signs hang on one door and only one person is busy. No-one can make a decision without the approval from the Party secretary.

With power concentrated in the hands of the town's Party secretary, the local government had become irrelevant. The influence of town leaders therefore depended on whether they were also members of the Party committee. The Party committee confined itself to political matters, provided supervision, and backing, for the town government while the principal responsibility of the town government was the administration of local affairs.

The town leadership consisted of three organisations. These were the standing committee of the local people's congress, the town Party committee, which comprised the Party secretary and deputy, committee members and clerks, and third, the town government. Constitutionally, the standing committee of the local people's congress was a supervisory body for the local administration. Its office was staffed by a chairman and vice-chairman who were responsible for major matters. The party committee, however, remained the highest authority in the town. Its branches extended into every village under the town's jurisdiction, and into every large company. The town government included the head and deputy head of the town, their offices, and the management departments for social and economic affairs. The town government had overall responsibility for industry, agriculture and forestry, as well as the execution of public policy at local level. Included within their portfolio of activities were township enterprise management, technology promotion, small river management, town market development, education, birth control, public health-care, labour export, civil administration, military recruitment, and all other matters that fell outside the jurisdiction of other organisations. The town government's grassroots organisation was the village committee, each of which had a head.

A key role of the town government was its management of township and village enterprises (TVEs). These enterprises handed over a fixed profit quota to the town government which, in return, provided legal, administrative and personnel services and guarantees. A major responsibility was the appointment or removal of enterprise bosses, a process which was carried out in consultation with the Party committee. The town government exerted authority over the non-agricultural population through its subsidiary organisations. Most of the non-agricultural population were in fact employees of the state, working in areas as diverse as finance and policing.

The town government thus occupied a pivotal role in the life of the community. It focused particularly on the management of Neiguan's town core and the larger villages because it was from these that the local government drew most of its tax revenue. The smaller villages, all of which were located outside the basin, also fell under the direct jurisdiction of the town government.

The villages were divided into cooperatives, of which there were over 140 in Neiguan. Every agricultural family was assigned to a cooperative. The cooperatives were formerly responsible for organising collective labour, but since the introduction of the household responsibility system (*baochandaohu*) their duties had changed. Individual farmers now handed over part of their production to the cooperative. They also took part in public works such as terrace building, which they organised and helped fund. The cooperative collected the public grain quota, managed agricultural machinery, which it rented out to individual farmers, and provided technical services. The cooperative was also responsible for the grass-roots implementation and enforcement of birth control policies.

In addition to their role as public servants many town officials were now involved with business activities. The secretary of Jinping village Party branch told us that his work as a village cadre put him at everybody's disposal, which left him little time with his own family. He was studying enterprise management and technology with a view to setting up his own factory, and he was confident that investment would be forthcoming. Once this was in place he intended to resign his duties to work full-time in business.

Demographic Aspects

In the 10 year period 1984 to 1993 the population of Neiguan had increased by about a third, from under 9,000 to 10,500. Natural growth, i.e. births, had added over 1000 people to the town's roster in this interval. Approximately 200 people were being born on average in Neiguan each year, with 35 dying. The one-child policy had not been very successful here, and each household had at least two children. The head of Dingxi Second People's Hospital, explained:

> There is a process to be gone through before people accept birth control. In general, people toe the line. It is a different matter for families without a male child. Only a minority of families have three children.

Family tradition and the practical needs of life in the countryside had all contributed to the demand to produce a male child.

The other factor responsible for population growth in Neiguan was in-migration. Because of its role as a trading centre Neiguan's population had historically possessed a significant transient element. Some of these newcomers would settle in the district. We were told that officially one sixth of the population of Neiguan town and its surrounding areas were immigrants, or descended from immigrants, and we found a significant split in migration patterns before and after 1949. Eight of the second generation migrant families we encountered in our survey traced their origin to other provinces while 15 families came from other parts of Dingxi county or further afield in Gansu. Some were economic refugees; one family had come to the area to escape conflict between Han and Hui people in Ningxia. Many came to trade and stayed on. After 1949, the flow of migrants slowed markedly: the newer arrivals came to Neiguan through marriage, work assignments or job reallocation. More recent arrivals were not only fewer in number but tended to come from shorter distances.

After 1958, however, the introduction of the household registration system tied people to one place. Officially, the movement of individuals was now virtually restricted to those getting married (although some individuals were apparently rusticated to the countryside during this period) and population movement virtually ceased in Neiguan. After the Cultural Revolution, migration resumed. More people came from the countryside to Neiguan's town core, while local people who were surplus to local labour needs, moved away in search of work. Throughout China the predominant migration flow is traditionally from places of lower to places of higher administration - from village to small town and from small town to county town. Given the opportunity, individuals may well move to their provincial capital or to the large cities in the coastal provinces. For people living in the countryside in our area, Neiguan was the first link in the chain. This is particularly the case for young women, who could become upwardly mobile through marriage. Each year many young women from the countryside were allowed to move into Neiguan's town core after marrying residents. For non-agricultural persons living near Neiguan, but who were not entitled to settle in the county town, permission to settle in Neiguan was perceived as an attractive proposition. But most people in this category changed only their personal household registration to the town, leaving their families in the countryside. From an individual's point of view such a move was obviously advantageous, although there were some tensions within Neiguan town because the continuous in-migration from the countryside increased the burden on the town's administrative, cultural and health-care services.

Upward migration was difficult to achieve because the urban migration of peasants was limited by quota. High school graduates usually looked for assignments in the local administration, hospital, bank branches or schools as a means of leaving the land. These new townspeople generally remained in close contact with their families in the countryside. Some travelled several kilometres daily to work in the town. Others stayed in public dormitories and returned to their homes for weekends or holidays. Beyond Neiguan, the next link in the chain was registration in Dingxi county town. A certain kudos was attached to county town household registration (holders were considered to be 'big shots' by Neiguan residents). Some resident holders remained in Dingxi for part of the working week, returning home once or twice a week by taxi.

In the second half of the 1980s, Dingxi county brought in new rules for urban registration within the newly introduced policy guidelines which were designed to speed up the development of the towns. These permitted anyone who was willing to pay 4,000 yuan, as a contribution to the county town's development, to live there. According to the head of Neiguan town's police station, by 1993 some 20 people had moved from Neiguan to the county town under these new regulations, and subsequently 20-30 persons had moved annually, changing their registration status in the process.

After 1979, economic reform brought a rapid population increase in the area as local enterprises began to draw farmers away from the land. In the 1980s and 1990s, increasing numbers of the local surplus labour force went to look for work outside the county and the province. The statistics show that, since 1990, over 3,000 local farmers from the town had moved away to find work, which left around 800 persons unemployed. The local authorities were trying to find ways to export this labour, mainly to other destinations within Gansu. The jobs available in the province were not appealing: most, such as coal mining, involved hard manual labour and were poorly paid. The majority of the migrant labourers were single young men hoping to save towards marriage, which in this locality could cost between 20,000 and 30,000 yuan. Such migrants were hampered by their lack of education and social connections: in general, migration was regarded as a last resort. During the survey we found that unlike farmers from other provinces, whose destinations were usually the big coastal cities, Neiguan people tended to move to Inner Mongolia, Xinjiang and the Hexi Corridor in Gansu. These areas were short of labour, generally not as poor as Dingxi, and living costs were lower. Migrants who were looking for temporary contract work but who were not seeking to change their household registration status were encouraged by their own town and county authorities because they reduced surplus labour pressure. However, locally there was no exact figure for people in this category.

One of our respondents, who worked part-time in the agricultural technology station, was very worried about his future. He expected the station to lay off staff, which would have meant seeking work elsewhere. He was thinking of trying Xifeng, in the east of Gansu, where he had a relative. But he was not confident of receiving any help, and feared that he might end up in the coal mines. Neiguan had little to offer in terms of earning money, he told us. A handful of local people had gone to Lanzhou and other big cities to do business and had been successful. They had become 'big shots' overnight. However they accounted for just a small proportion of those who had left to seek work.

Many of those we spoke to had considered going elsewhere to seek financial rewards but the prospect was not an appealing one for them. Most would be content to remain in Neiguan provided they could get a job, and feed and clothe themselves. Only 12 per cent of respondents expressed any desire to move to another province or to settle in one of the major cities. Women, and adults over 40 years generally, felt the cities to be alien places where country people could be easily exploited. They felt it was better to stay amongst their own kind. Even younger respondents often felt they did not have the skills necessary to compete in the urban environment.

Statistical records show that the number of people from other provinces who moved to and settle down in Neiguan was extremely small. A very small group arrived from Wenzhou, Zhejiang province and worked in beekeeping, and quilt and furniture making. Another incomer was a tailor from Shaanxi province. Additionally, 20-30 itinerant traders from other provinces regularly came to do business, especially during the country fairs.

In recent years, household size was typically four or five persons, reflecting a trend in family structure from extended to nuclear. In the 1990 census the average household size was 4.7 persons. The average number of persons in the households we surveyed in our study was 5.3. (Household members were defined in terms of those who slept and eat in the same place and who consulted on household matters together.) Forty-four per cent of households contained 4-5 persons and 41 per cent of households contained six or more members. Only two per cent of households contained 10 persons or more. The ratio of males to females in the households surveyed was almost exactly 1:1. Households of between four and six persons were quite common in Neiguan, as elsewhere in rural inland China. These typically comprised a young couple with one or two children and one, or even both sets of parents. In such families it was generally the young couple who were working to provide the economic support for the household. Because country residents did not have pensions, people who were past working age depended on the support of their children. Households with seven or more members in one family usually consisted of one or two great grandparents, one or more grandparents, and a young couple with their offspring, and perhaps unmarried young relatives of the same generation as themselves. Family authority usually reverted to able-bodied, middle-aged grandparents. Their children, married or not, still deferred to them. This structure tended to provoke conflict, however, particularly between in-laws. The unwritten rule in this situation was that the next person to get married left the family house.

Income and Work

Income

'Money' was the word we heard most in Neiguan. Making money and 'finding money' (*zhao qian*) were frequent topics of conversation. Farmers talked of the possibility of commercial pig farming and cash cropping. Cadres from the township enterprises made plans to persuade the banks to lend them money for fresh developments. Local officials talked of inward investment, including the possibility of attracting foreign capital. Clearly, the traditional view that money is a source of evil had been discarded.

In 1983, a few years into the era of economic reform, the reported per capita income was just 74 yuan per year. Between 1990 and 1993, annual per capita income in Neiguan increased from 500 to 807 yuan, an increase of 12 per cent. According to the secretary of the town's Party committee, the per capita income for 1994 was over 750 yuan. Poverty households (*kunnan hu*) in Neiguan accounted for 10 per cent of the total. Another 10 per cent had an annual income over 10,000 yuan. The secretary of the Party in Neiguan told us that in his own village annual income was nearly 800 yuan per head, five per cent of households suffered food shortages, but there were 60 television sets.

Average income to households included in our survey was around 4,600 yuan in 1994, equivalent to 860 yuan per head. However, around 14 per cent of households had an annual income of less than 2,000 yuan and 15 per cent received over 7,000 yuan. The largest group of households, just over a fifth, earned between 2000 and 3000 yuan. On average nearly half of total household income came from agriculture and sideline production, around 30 per cent as wages, and just over 13 per cent came from other commercial activities. The individual respondents in our survey had an average annual income of approximately 1,900 yuan. Nearly half of them claimed they were satisfied with this level of income.

The household survey found that family income came from diverse sources. For example, the deputy-head of the town had six members in his family, including two children in school and two elderly parents. His own wage income was between 3,000 and 4,000 yuan annually. The family kept four pigs for commercial purposes, which earned him a further 3,000 yuan. The family also had 25 mu of responsibility crop land (*zeren tian*) and in the previous year had sold 6,000 jin of grain for over 1,000 yuan. They also harvested 7,000 jin of potatoes, of which 5,000 were sold for over 2000 yuan. In addition, they grew over 1,000 jin of dry rice for use as animal feed. This gave the family a total income of over 9,000 yuan in the most recent year. Even without a wage income, family earnings still reached 5,000-6,000 yuan annually. Given sufficient application, agriculture and sideline production could exceed, rather than just supplement, salary income.

Overall, the living standards of Neiguan's farmers were still at the *wenbao* level (adequate in food and clothing). But adequacy was itself a great improvement on comparatively recent times. In a high proportion of households most income was still spent on food. Two families we visited, each with an average standard of living, lived almost entirely on a diet of noodles and fresh or preserved vegetables. Such a diet was typical for the area. Meat and fish would only be consumed in any quantity at New Year, with leftovers from the banquet being salted and stored. New Year was also the only time for many people when clothing was bought. Even people who would be at the fashion conscious age elsewhere were dressed in military cast-offs and *zhongshan* cotton clothes, that is what Westerners refer to as Mao tunics. It was common for newly wealthy families to put money towards new housing. During our stay, the secretary of Neiguan village Party branch was in the middle of building his new house, a bungalow with three or four rooms. The cost was said to be around 1,500 yuan. This seemed very little, probably because the family made their own construction materials such as bricks and concrete beams.

Agriculture

Around 93 per cent of working people in Neiguan were involved in agriculture. Also many of those who worked full time in industry and commerce retained an interest in farming. In our survey, for example, 77 per cent of respondents had their own grain supply. The main crops on the terraced loess were wheat, peas, broad beans, and potatoes. Flax, mustard seed, hemp, dangshen (*Codonopsis pilosula*) and Chinese angelica were also grown as cash crops. Most of the farm work was done manually, with the assistance of oxen and mules.

Crop yield in this region is highly sensitive to moisture availability during the growing season. However, all the officials we met claimed that the agricultural reforms of the 1980s, particularly the introduction of the household responsibility system in the early 1980s, had brought substantial improvements in yield, and thus to the lives of local farmers. Agricultural productivity is increasing yearly, we were told, except during drought years, or in those years when a major flood or hailstorm occurred during the growing season. By 1993, annual per capita grain production had reached 466 kilograms, providing an income of 689 yuan. Neiguan's grain production was usually at the top of Dingxi county's productivity tables. Also, land-use had diversified, with cash cropping, animal husbandry and forestry becoming increasingly prominent. Because of its status as a designated pilot town, Neiguan had made an earlier start than most others in the area in diversifying its agricultural economy. One third of its land was now used for cash crops, the output of which reputedly increased by a factor of four between 1983 and 1993. We were told that the average annual rate of increase in grain production was 0.4 per cent over the same period. Potatoes were now grown in sufficient quantity for a surplus to be sold for starch processing. Certain villages had also been designated as orchard centres. At household level, farmers were encouraged to turn over gardens and empty lots around the village for small-scale market gardening, fruit growing and vegetable and mushroom production. Commercial crops accounted for a quarter of agricultural output and the town leadership appeared determined to increase this proportion. There were further plans to establish orchards, increase vegetable production and develop processing industries. Ironically, the household responsibility system which made these changes possible initially, was blamed for holding back their development. According to an official in Dingxi's government office:

> The household-based method is not the way ahead. We need to broaden vegetable production, and there is also the issue of how to fully utilise flax after its oil is extracted for food consumption. And there is more potential for starch processing. None of these has been developed yet.

In his opinion, agriculture should be treated as a platform for township industries.

Each household had a livestock target of four pigs and ten chickens. A further fifteen families had been designated specialist cattle rearers: they kept at least four animals, three of them for commercial supply. But not all livestock production was on such a small scale. Close to Neiguan's town core we interviewed a pig farmer with over 100 animals. He was also a fairly substantial employer with 37 farmhands. He was an

AN ENTREPRENEURIAL FARMER

This 29 year-old was a rare commodity in Neiguan - a senior high school graduate. He was well off, but wanted to do even better. So far, a few of his schemes had failed.

In my second year of senior middle school I started to date a girl and my marks went downhill. After graduating I got married, and a terrible thing happened: when the army came recruiting, they wouldn't look at a married man. I suffer from the peasant way of looking at the world. When I started doing business on my own account, I chose to sell clothing, but round here people only buy at the Spring Festival. So I turned to the transport business. It was OK but later fuel and various taxes became too much. So I sold my vehicle and went into trading rapeseed. Sometimes you could make 100 yuan a day. After Liberation my family was classed as 'rich peasant'. But my father hadn't any schooling and just herded sheep. My second uncle was clever and did business such as selling pigs in Lanzhou before 1949. Now he is back to business, making potato noodles; his son-in-law transports coal.

As for me, this year I've had to abandon thoughts of business as my wife goes out to work. But I'm thinking of setting up a company dealing in building materials. I had this idea last year, as one of my neighbours did it. He sells plaster boards for ceilings and made 20-30,000 yuan last year. My brother and I would need 4-5,000 yuan to get going. Now the farmers round here all go for plaster board for their ceilings and there's a good market. In Neiguan, if you want to borrow from the bank you first of all have to have close, special relations with the bank people. This is the case with 70 per cent of those who get money. But the bank won't offer me a loan because they think I'm too young to be trustworthy.

enthusiastic student of modern pig farming methods, keen to shorten the fattening period and raise farrowing and piglet survival rates. As a sideline, he processed 30,000 kilograms of starch per year, using the waste to feed to his animals.

The town leadership was attempting to lower the vulnerability of crop production to natural disasters and to increase local knowledge about modern techniques and technology. Specific measures included building and maintaining terraced fields, large-scale tree and grass planting, the introduction of higher yielding crop varieties, and even the establishment of three artillery pieces on local hillsides to disperse hailstorms by 'cloudbusting'. Agriculture certainly remained a cornerstone of the Neiguan economy, but the target of grain self sufficiency - 'grain as the key link' - appeared to have been firmly set aside.

Industry and Commerce

At the start of the reform period Neiguan's economy was overwhelmingly agricultural. There were few other activities apart from the kilns and repair shops which served the needs of the local farming community. However, these enterprises provided the town with the nucleus for the development of a township industry sector which was a key element in the economic reforms of the early 1980s. At first, township enterprises were regarded as a means of absorbing Neiguan's surplus labour force, which totalled about 6,000 persons in the early 1980s. Later, their economic benefits became apparent, and after 1985 a stream of new enterprises was set up, including factories for bleach powder, starch products and polypropylene fibre. The rapid development of township industry in Neiguan was rather chaotic and many enterprises were unsuccessful. This is reflected in the data: between 1983 and 1990 the number of factories grew from 11 to 150. By the 1990s, however, the number of factory enterprises fell to 40. In the mid-1990s these employed about 2,250 people, produced 70 million yuan in output value, and contributed annually almost one million yuan to the local government in taxes. The largest, and seemingly the most stable and viable of these, were run by the township government itself.

Neiguan has a poor natural resource base for enterprise development. Most raw materials were imported, and the products were exported to neighbouring provinces. The local planners referred to this system as '*liang tou zai wai*' ('two heads outside'). Some people we spoke to felt that Neiguan should pay more attention to its own, albeit limited, resources. One suggestion we heard was that Neiguan should set up some crop processing factories based on local produce, flax processing for example. Another suggestion was that Neiguan could process locally grown soya beans, broad beans and peas for China's rapidly developing 'health food' market.

Township enterprises were the main source of government revenue. In addition, they absorbed surplus labour and boosted the cash economy. The majority of our respondents, many of whom would have stood to gain by new employment opportunities, felt there was a need for more TVEs, while town officials emphasised the key role of TVEs as a source of revenue from taxation. The town leadership had adopted a strategy of encouraging the wealthier farmers and existing cooperatives to pool investment in new factories and in upgrading technology in existing ones. However, the town government was gradually withdrawing its direct involvement in factory management and limiting itself to providing legal, personnel and administrative services.

The biggest township enterprise in Neiguan was the Nuanquan Industrial Company. This enterprise was established in 1977 and achieved company status in 1988. It had issued stock since 1994. Originally the company employed 40 people, engaged in the production of poor quality plastic goods for a virtually non-existent market. Its survival depended entirely on government subsidies and bank loans. The company's first proper commercial contract, with the Lanzhou Oil Chemical Company, was effected by Neiguan people living in Lanzhou, the provincial capital. The company had subsequently diversified into polypropylene fibres, industrial filter cloths and similar materials. It operated from four sites and had successfully developed a supply chain to some of Gansu's leading plastics and textiles companies. In 1994, the company paid over 16 million yuan to the local government in taxes. In the same year it changed its ownership structure through a private share issue. The company itself held 40 per cent of the stock. Nearly all the employees were also shareholders.

Nanquan and the other township enterprises accounted for over three quarters of the town's revenue. Electricity supplies to outlying villages, road construction in the countryside and agricultural investment were all paid for by the town government whose revenue was largely dependent upon the profits made by the town's enterprises. However, a complaint we repeatedly heard from town officials was that much of the taxation provided to the town had to be passed upwards to the county level administration.

Enterprises at village level and below had also expanded, although their development was patchy. In one village, five local enterprises consolidated to form the Five Star Company which had an annual income of nearly one million yuan in the mid-1990s. Neiguan's 448 household enterprises registered a collective yearly profit of around 670,000 yuan.

Although economic development in Neiguan was still largely government run, private developments had also been impressive. Two examples from the hundred or so business people in Neiguan are mentioned here. One, a 48 year-old businessman, was among the wealthiest people in the town. His mannerisms and general outlook conveyed the impression of a shrewd businessman. Before 1949 he worked in coal mines near Lanzhou, rising from labourer to foreman. Having earned some money, he returned home, invested in land and studied herbal medicine. After 1949, he went 'underground'. By day he would work for a local collective farm. In his spare time he set up a clandestine trading operation, importing corduroy from Xi'an and selling it in town. In 1964, he was accused of speculation, his house was ransacked, his stock confiscated and he was fined. For the remainder of the Cultural Revolution he was forced to be a bricklayer in his commune construction team, which compared to many similarly charged was a relatively lenient punishment. He then re-started his clothing business, which had earned him around 3,000 yuan per year and had allowed him to amass considerable savings. Another businessman, once vilified for private trading, now had big plans to expand into industry. He intended to set up an instant noodle factory as a subsidiary for a Beijing based company which offered to inject 160,000 yuan into the project and to take its entire output. He intended to invest 80,000 yuan of his own money, using his wife's and his uncle's properties as collateral. He told us he was now seeking a third investment to put his plan into effect. His overtures to the town government to invest in similar schemes in the past had been rejected.

Neiguan's long history as a trading centre is referred to earlier in this chapter, and the tradition was clearly extant. The market in Neiguan's town-core area attracted farmers and traders from throughout Dingxi and surrounding counties. A variety of goods were on sale and there were specialised markets for grain, timber, medicinal materials and livestock. On occasions, as many as 20,000 people crowded into the centre of the town, thereby doubling its normal population. More typically, market days attracted around 7000 people. The various town and village markets were supposed to pay for improvements in local roads and in water and electricity supply. However, traders were often unwilling to use designated areas for their activities, with the result that revenue was insufficient to match the cost of such improvements.

The majority of Neiguan's urban residents were employed by the state, reflecting Neiguan's role as the political, cultural and health-care centre of the district. For example, most of the 80 or so health workers in the County's Second People's Hospital in Neiguan held town household registrations. Similarly, most of the 100 teaching staff at the Second County Middle School were non-rural in registration.

THE TOWN'S DEPUTY CHIEF

This 40 year-old's main task within Neiguan's government structure was to foster and develop the township and village enterprises. (He was known to be plain speaking and entrepreneurial.)

I come from Yongfeng and graduated from Beijing Economics College through a correspondence course. I used to be the Communist youth league secretary, and then the Party secretary in the village. In 1983 I was transferred to the town's brick kiln as its deputy director. The following year I was the director. In 1985 I was transferred to a supply cooperative to be Party secretary. In 1987 I was transferred again, being made Party secretary of the plastics factory belonging to the Nanquan Company. I was there for three years. In 1991 there was a lot of reorganisation and the Enterprise Management Association was set up; I was appointed chief. A year later I got my present position.

The collective enterprises in Neiguan have developed OK over the past few years. But there are a few problems: funds are insufficient, debts are too heavy. The banking system has been revamped so it's much harder to get credit. The burden on the enterprises can be great, and this makes them difficult to manage. Without these enterprises it's difficult to develop the town as a whole. Private businesses have been springing up lately - they can get going quickly but at high risk and are usually more efficient than collective ones. The traditional way of controlling enterprises is a problem: they were thought of as part of the government system and so no real pressures can be exerted. This will all change if shareholding is brought in and enterprises are pushed towards the market. They can then sink or swim....

As far as the environment is concerned, great changes have taken place here. During the time of the people's communes, much of the land was terraced. When the responsibility system came in (in the mid-1980s) it was stopped for a while, but then terracing started again in earnest. The money comes out of the grain and construction fees from the State Council. A lot of tree planting took place especially in the early 1980s and the town government invested about 100,00 yuan a year. It went on until the communes were abolished. Now the town government has no money and not a lot is being spent. And people are continually chopping down the trees and this is getting worse and worse. The awareness of the environment is very poor. Now all we can do is rely on fines but they can't solve the problem.

Environmental Issues

Natural Hazards - Drought

Our stays in Neiguan mainly coincided with the dry winter period, in years when rainfall amounts were well below average. The problem of water supply was immediately obvious, and was expressed at an anecdotal level as well as by the official statistics. Exposed river beds, which were covered with saline deposits, were being used as a thoroughfare for tractors, or as a playground for children. During one of our visits, we stayed in the guesthouse of the bank, which was situated opposite the headquarters of the town government. Even the 40 metre deep well inside the government compound had dried up. Every day we walked 200 metres to the local hospital to fetch water. And we used water economically. Rather than climb five flights of stairs with full buckets, we would use the same water to wash ourselves and our clothes before using it to flush the toilet. We knew theoretically what water shortages entailed. Now we had some direct experience of what it was like to live under these conditions. Neiguan's reputation for being 'on top of the world for regional poverty' had a strong resonance. These images, however, contrast strongly with those portrayed in one ancient poem: 'standing on the West Bridge, barely seeing the rainbow through the dense willow trees, joining the Nuanquan river were the clear waters from the four streams.' In the eyes of this ancient poet, Neiguan was as beautiful and fertile as *Jiangnan*, the south bank of the Yangzi. More prosaically, apparently Neiguan was once a well watered and forested place.

Certainly, Neiguan's position in a basin should mean that the town is naturally well sited for water supply. In fact Neiguan's natural water resources were better than other parts of Dingxi county. According to the director of Neiguan's agriculture technology station, water shortages were a comparatively recent phenomenon in the Neiguan area. Even as recently as the 1970s, he told us, water flowed in the local rivers throughout the year while the larger rivers supported fish populations. More recently, a progressive reduction in river flow, and its cessation during dry intervals, had necessitated well-digging in order to access aquifer water. However, the wells dug in the mid 1980s had since dried up, so deeper wells were required. Over-exploitation of both surface and aquifer water, exacerbated by a series of low rainfall years, had resulted in a very serious situation. The secretary of the town's Party committee summarised the situation:

Even the best-watered places have problems now; wells are being dug deeper and deeper and water is still getting harder and harder to find. Surface water is nowhere to be found.

It is estimated that in recent years the underground water level had been dropping by as much as one metre annually. In Jinping village, for example, wells were 13 metres deep and we were told that in some other villages 20 metre deep wells were not unusual. The situation was so bad in Xiaguan and Dongguan villages that families were forced to buy water.

We found Neiguan inhabitants to be very sensitive to the issue of water supply, and there was a consensus that the situation was worsening. Local cadres commented that yearly amounts of rainfall had declined markedly since the mid-1980s, so much so that most years were now designated 'drought years'. However this has not always been the case. According to the local records, over the 931 years from the Song dynasty to 1946, only 29 droughts were recorded, an average of one every 30 years. Twelve of these were described as severe. Eight droughts took place in the 35 years from 1921 to 1946. But between 1950 and 1974, there were 17 droughts, at a frequency of one every 18 months. Eight of these were classed as a major drought. No rain fell during a six month period in 1993. Although the term 'drought' may be variously defined, and it is difficult to establish a consistent long-term drought record, there is strong circumstantial evidence that annual rainfall amounts had declined since the 1950s. In addition to having a major influence on crop productivity, water shortages were a major problem for owners of livestock.

Low lying cropland, previously irrigated by surface water was now supplied by subterranean water. In the decades before the household responsibility system was introduced, the pumps were collective property, but they were now subcontracted to farmers, who in turn hired them out to others. The fees levied were intended to pay for the cost of maintenance, repair, management, and the labour to operate the pumps. The need to upgrade pumps in order to draw water from increasing depth had caused a sharp rise in fees. In 1981, 1.8 yuan was needed to irrigate one mu of land. By 1994, the cost had increased to between 10 and 12 yuan. The fields on local farms had to be watered three times a year, twice in summer and once in winter. Based on eight mu of paddy per household, it thus required 240 yuan a year to irrigate all of the land. The cost of pumping water had threatened the economic viability of irrigated farming in the Neiguan basin. Water price increases had to be paid for from surplus wheat sold on the market. If yields fell due to crop disease or insect outbreaks, both of which occur periodically, then the farmer risked being unable to pay for the next round of irrigation. Without irrigation, families would not be able to produce wheat either for sale or for personal consumption.

One aspect of the water problem was succinctly captured by a dispute we witnessed between farmers and the pump contractor in Xiafeng village. The cause of the dispute was a proposed increase in the water price; it was the wheat sowing season, and the pump was out of order. The contractor was demanding more money for repairs but the farmers felt they had already paid enough. Eventually the local authority was called in and we saw a town official mediating in the dispute. One of the farmers involved told us:

> Water is getting so expensive, we can earn almost nothing, but what else can we do? If we don't grow crops, we can't feed ourselves. And we can't buy food, because we have no money.

In many rural dwellings in Neiguan, particularly on the dry loess hills, water was collected and stored in *shuijiao*, simple underground water storage systems. These structures, which had the appearance of wells, held several tonnes of water. They were fed only by rainwater run-off. Rainfall events were few in this region, so it was essential to harvest the available water as efficiently as possible. The *shuijiao* were situated at the lowest point of the courtyards of farmsteads and homes. The well opening was fed by rainwater which ran off the roofs on three sides of the courtyard and on to the sloping, tamped-down courtyard surface and into the well opening. In fact the roofs were asymmetrical in order to maximise the water harvesting area. The World Bank had recently supported a programme of concreting courtyards, which significantly reduced water losses from the surface.

Traditionally, local farmers had turned to rather less certain activities in an attempt to increase water availability. At the top of each of the hills immediately to the east of the town there was a man-made earth pile, about a dozen metres high. For centuries, these had been used as sacrificial altars by local farmers. Whenever a drought occurred they would come here to make offerings and oblations as well as to pray for rain.

The shortage of water resources also prevented Neiguan's growing TVE sector from reaching its full potential and will doubtless act as a constraint to further developments. Operations could be suspended, for example, because of interruptions in flow. The assistant Party secretary for Dingxi county emphasised the pivotal role of water supply for future industrial developments. He wanted to target those industries with relatively low water requirements. This view was reinforced by the Party secretary of the Dingxi county committee who told us:

> Per capita water share here is below the national average. Industry needs water. To solve the conflict, we have adopted a series of measures. The first is to avoid high water consuming projects and to develop low water consuming industries and to set up household courtyard water-saving projects.

In order to enhance water availability and to reduce the attendant risks of flooding and erosion, Gansu province initiated the 'Yintao' project in the 1950s. The idea was to divert water from the Tao River, which flows to the south of Dingxi, into the central region of the province where thirteen counties experienced severe drought. Initial attempts were abandoned due to economic and technical constraints, with great financial loss. The project was resumed in 1992 after several feasibility studies conducted in the 1980s. We met the vice-chairman of the Chinese people's political consultative conference of Gansu province. He was a local man and served as director of the original project. He told us that the project would bring enormous benefits to Neiguan, and the town's future development depended upon it. Unfortunately the project's great cost, an estimated four billion yuan, meant that it had been suspended indefinitely.

Other Natural Hazards

While water is normally scarce in Neiguan, rainfall events can be of high intensity. The gullies and alluvial fans, and the broken branches and boulder-strewn river beds, were testimony to the power of flowing water in this usually dry landscape. When rainfall is excessive, water from the local hills cascades into the town. One such event, which caused the worse flooding since 1949, occurred shortly before one of our visits. Some parts of Neiguan town were under half a metre of water, causing houses and walls to collapse. It was believed locally that the situation was exacerbated by the failure to maintain water conservancy facilities and that some of these may have been deliberately sabotaged. One local farmer commented:

> Neiguan's rivers and wooded areas used to be in very good shape; flooding happened but it was rare. All his life, my father only saw two floods. There was a big flood in 1994 which burst the dyke. My kitchen and garden walls were flattened by the flood. But the water didn't stay; it joined the Nuanquan river and went away to the county town of Dingxi.

The flooding happens because the trees planted on the river banks during the commune years have all been cut down, together with the roots.

We were told that widespread deforestation took place on the loess hills in the post-1949 era and rapidly accelerated during the years of the Great Leap Forward when wood was needed to fuel the furnaces. It was widely perceived locally that the loss of tree cover had led to an increased intensity of flooding and to a general decline in rainfall. Certainly we would anticipate more rapid run off of water, and perhaps less recharge of aquifers with deforestation. However, it is more difficult to support the latter claim.

Pollution

Pollution issues were the concern of the environmental protection section of Dingxi county's urban construction bureau. This section, created in 1989, developed from the former sanitation section which employed just one person for cleansing and waste disposal. At the time of our visit the environmental protection section had eight staff: two were graduates and four others had some high school education. The section head had some higher education, having trained in horticulture at Shanghai's University of Science and Technology, although he did not graduate. There was also an environmental test station locally, but we were told it was inadequately staffed and equipped. The environmental protection section had responsibility for some 140 manufacturing enterprises in Dingxi county, of which about 80 belonged to the townships. Their main work was in monitoring air pollution, we were told, although some time was also spent on water pollution issues. Formerly the section was involved in tree planting and other measures, but rapid industrialisation had resulted in a cessation of these activities.

Departments of environmental protection were supposed to have the final word over new developments. In practice they seemed to have limited influence in Dingxi. The head of the section told us that industrial plant could be set up without his unit being informed. Indeed, it was common for the environmental protection section not to be informed of new developments. A factory producing asphalt had already begun construction and received 400,000 yuan in investment before it came to the notice of the local environmental authorities. Permission to build had been granted through other channels, and the environmental department, despite legitimate concerns about the carcinogenic effects of asphalt, was powerless. A particular problem for environmental protection was the arrival of polluting industries which would have been forbidden in Lanzhou, even though that metropolis was one of the most heavily polluted places in China. For example, the environmental authorities were unable to prevent the relocation of a polluting nickel battery factory from Lanzhou. Also, in Neiguan's development zone, which was established without reference to the environmental authorities, there were several chemical factories, including a fertiliser plant. Contrary to environmental protection rules, this was located on the windward side of the town. A major problem was the lack of liaison between the economic planning department and the environmental protection authorities, although it was not difficult to understand the former's motives. The problem was exacerbated by the county government's refusal to allow its environmental protection staff to intervene. Sometimes, environmental workers were treated with open contempt. Following the market liberalisation measures of 1992, an enterprise-building frenzy swept through Dingxi and most of the town's green spaces were built upon. Local environmental protection staff who remonstrated with the work units responsible were simply told that they had no recourse in law.

So while the environmental protection authorities should, in principle, have been informed about the possible polluting effects of new projects sponsored by the county government, and should also have been able to influence the final decision over their acceptance, in practice this was not the case. They believed the county government simply regarded environmental workers as a nuisance. The head of environmental protection in Dingxi county claimed that his office would have more power if it were to be constituted as a department in itself, able to deal directly with the local planning committee, rather than as a subsidiary body of the urban construction committee. Other problems for environmental protection in Dingxi county were too few staff, inadequately trained staff, and too little time for further training. The overwhelming impression was that economic benefits always outweighed the environmental costs. Nonetheless, the head of the environmental section claimed some positive influences on the town's development, including a heightened awareness of environmental issues through the dissemination of information about national laws on environmental protection, by organising training courses for factory managers on environmental subjects, and by publishing guidelines on environmental protection for local enterprises. The environmental section also played a role in mediating and solving legal cases that arose from pollution incidents.

Because of its importance within Dingxi county, Neiguan had its own urban construction office. One of its staff told us that she was involved with a variety of issues, but mainly with environmental protection. One of her tasks was to deal with applications for new buildings (discussed further below); another was to manage Neiguan's market, a perennial problem because of the waste generated and the general chaos on market days. This informant was in no doubt that environmental issues had been paid too little attention in Neiguan. Despite the priority accorded industrial developments, the vice-director of Neiguan *zhen* told us that the town's plan for a pulp and paper factory had been vetoed at county level because the inevitable discharges into water courses would have caused problems downstream. While acknowledging the benefits of environmental protection, Neiguan's vice-director clearly prioritised the development of industry because to him it was the only way the town could develop economically and also solve the surplus labour problem.

Our initial impression of Neiguan was that the local environment was relatively free from pollution. The air seemed clear, certainly much more so than in China's large urban centres, and the local drinking water, which was mainly from underground sources, was clean and without any aftertaste. This view was corroborated by our respondents: just over 90 per cent rated the air as 'clear' and 85 per cent described their drinking water as 'good' or 'very good'. However, there were some conspicuous problems. The town had an open drainage system, but fly-tipping by local enterprises had blocked the drains, creating pools of dirty water which spilled over the main road after rain, making passage difficult for vehicles and people. The rubbish included debris from an informal vegetable market sited in front of the local hospital. Local people were highly critical of the sanitation problem this had created. There was other visible evidence of local pollution sources. Powder dust from the bleach factory coated the adjacent cropland with white powder. This factory was also the source of a major chlorine leak a few years prior to our visit. Although this was apparently an isolated incident, leaks continued to be a potential hazard. In addition, untreated waste water was discharged from the flour processing plant, although with treatment this material could have been used as a fertiliser. Another cause of complaint was the waste water released from a glass fibre factory into one of the town's open ditches.

Although the pollution problem in Dingxi was less palpable than in China's cities, the problem was growing as local industries developed. The county town of Dingxi occupied only 6.5 square kilometres, but within this small area there were 400 non-domestic coal burning boilers and heating systems: the result was that local air quality was amongst the worst in Gansu province. The main problem was the absence of a power plant for the whole town. Thus, each work-unit had its own coal-fired boiler, over 100 of which emitted more gases than permitted by official guidelines. In the larger area of Dingxi county, untreated waste was released from 25 factories, 15 of which belonged to the county government. Together they emitted around three million tonnes of waste water each year. A paper factory was a particularly bad source of pollution, including some highly toxic substances. Much of its waste was dumped into a stream which was used as a source of water for farm animals. Although it is always difficult to establish cause-effect relationships in such cases, the perception of the environmental protection section head was that the water was responsible for sterility and miscarriages in animals. But because the factory was profitable the county government had ring-fenced it from further attentions by environmental protection staff. The director of Dingxi county's urban construction bureau told us that most of the local industrial processes relied on old technology, and that this resulted in high pollution outputs in relation to productivity. The situation would only change, he said, if new technology was installed, which would require investment on a scale the county could not afford.

A recent chlorine leak from the bleach powder factory in Neiguan provided an example of the rather pragmatic way the environmental protection process worked. Farmers affected by the leak reported the incident to the county's environment protection section, whose staff then visited the factory and conducted tests. They concluded that chlorine poisoning had killed 120 pigs and caused 20,000 yuan worth of damage. The victims asked the factory to pay 50 per cent of the damage, but the factory, pleading its inability to meet such costs, paid only 6,000 yuan. To resolve the issue the town government found a new location for the pig farm, at a greater distance from the factory. According to the local environmental protection section, the pollution from the factory remained very serious, a view confirmed by local people. However, we obtained another perspective on the chlorine incident from the manager of the factory, who discussed it with us at some length. While accepting that his factory was the source of the leak, he claimed it was due to the workers being unfamiliar with recently installed technology, and that the effects of the leak were worsened by strong winds and a power cut. He reminded us that chlorine gas, being heavier than air, was not easily dispersed, but on this occasion the strong winds had carried it to the surrounding fields, 'burning' the crops. However, he believed some people had used the incidence for their own ends, claiming that the level of damage to the wheat crop had been exaggerated by farmers in an attempt to boost their compensation. Furthermore, the factory manager remained unconvinced that the chlorine leak was to blame for the death of the pigs, citing as evidence an epidemic which the farm was experiencing at the time and the fact that other nearby pig farms were unaffected. Nonetheless, the factory had paid proper compensation for the losses incurred, and for the transfer of the affected farm, and apparently controls had been tightened in the factory as a result of the incident.

While incidents of this sort show the less desirable aspects of industrialisation, the pollution here was relatively low compared with those regions where township industry was much more developed. Certainly, the topic of pollution was much less discussed by both officials and the public than the problem of water scarcity. In our survey we explored a number of environmental issues with the respondents. Overall we found a reasonably high level of satisfaction with the local environment: around 60 per cent of respondents rated the town core environment 'good' or 'very good'. Most ordinary villagers thought the town was reasonably attractive. Complaints came from a small number of interviewees who tended to be the younger and better educated residents and perhaps compared conditions with bigger, better organised places, or simply had been sensitised to environmental issues by the media. Everyone identified Neiguan's main environmental problems as water shortage and poor sanitation. The chlorine spillage incident mentioned above was referred to by only 20 per cent of respondents. A similarly low proportion of respondents was aware of the local environmental protection organisations and only half of these respondents understood the nature of their work. Some respondents, however, believed the county authorities were over-concerned with economic development, and gave too little attention to environmental protection. One commented:

> Many big factories with pollution problems were forced out of Lanzhou and have been given permission to move to Dingxi; the local authorities are only interested in investment and increased revenues; by the time our department finds out about the projects all the necessary procedures have been completed.

Another commented at length:

Setting up industries here which are discarded from other places is not the way forward; when industries like this are moved here, they still do not have environmental protection measures, so in the long run it is not worthwhile to have them here. Take the waterproof materials plant: compare how much it earns in a year with the damage it causes to the health of Dingxi people; the asphalt they make can cause cancer, but this problem only surfaces ten years on. Officials here only look at short-term benefits; who cares about problems that may occur ten years later? It would be better if they thought about both economic and environment benefits.

The issue of exporting dirty industries from large cities to small towns was raised by many residents, many of whom cited as an example the local bleach factory. Interestingly, staff of the county's environmental protection section claimed that local people were not very conscious of, or concerned about, environmental issues. And indeed, some respondents did put development first and the environment a poor second, as is evident from the following quotation from a respondent:

We understand the importance of environmental protection, but our business is small and needs to develop. Here, the majority want economic development and we have to listen to them. If this causes pollution then we can come back and handle it later. For us, development and environment are both important issues. But the former is more important. Meeting basic living requirements like food is still a problem for some of us here.

One of our questions concerned the acceptability of polluting factories in the *zhen*, but with the prospect of higher incomes. Fifty-seven per cent of respondents believed this to be acceptable, but 36 per cent believed it to be unacceptable. Similarly, 55 per cent of respondents claimed they would take a job even though it was known to be hazardous to health.

While environmental issues might not be expected to be given high priority for those who have few material comforts, we found that both officials and the general public in Neiguan were conscious of environmental issues, particularly as they affected their private lives and public business. This consciousness was most developed in the younger and better educated respondents. Furthermore this environmental concern was not restricted to local issues, but extended to the national, and in some cases, to the global arena.

Land Loss

In such an ecologically fragile area as southern Gansu there were cogent reasons for strict zoning and land management regulations. Our key informant on land issues was the director of the land management bureau of Dingxi county. His unit has responsibility for 36 *zhen* and *xiang*, although three *zhen*, including Neiguan, had their own branch and others had a single officer. Within the bureau the land construction branch dealt with applications for construction, another branch dealt with issues of land quality, including financial aspects, and another had responsibility for monitoring the implementation of regulations concerning land-use changes. We were told that 'strict rules' governed land-use and management in Dingxi county, and that detailed measures were in place to deal with the protection and rational use of crop land. According to the bureau, if as little as one mu of land was taken out of production, another had to be developed to compensate for the loss. Anyone, or any organisation involved in a project that required a change of land-use was supposed to submit a formal application. Those involved in unofficial land-use changes, whether as individuals or at the village level, were fined. We were told that one village in Neiguan was made to pay over 200,000 yuan for converting 78 mu of crop land without permission. Official regulations were reinforced by regular inspections, but to a large extent it was assumed that the strict land laws would be adhered to on trust. Inspectors looked for breaches of the three 'nos' (*sanwu*), i.e. no illegal use, no use in excess of permission and no over-occupation of crop land. Villages which complied were apparently awarded with a *sanwu* plate at a public ceremony while offending villages had any such awards withdrawn to shame them into compliance.

A particular problem for the bureau was the demand from newly wealthy peasants for land for houses. In theory, planning permission was required from both the town and the county authorities, and only vacant, uncultivated land was meant to be used. But it cost 300 yuan to make an application. People unwilling to part with their money and wait for official approval simply built their houses. Once discovered, the authorities, so we were told, were empowered to pull the houses down. Despite this rather drastic action, the demand for new housing was so great that it was difficult to contain the problem. When permission to build a new house was granted, county government regulations stipulated a maximum floor area of 200 square metres, including courtyard. The director of the land management bureau conceded this was not really sufficient for farmers because they required additional buildings for pigs and sheep. In most cases, it seemed the farmers simply built to their requirements, as long as good farm land was not occupied.

The land management bureau was also involved in publicity campaigns to promote the land regulations. Local leaders were targeted because it was felt that their understanding of the issues would better promote compliance. According to the director of the land management bureau many cadres were still ignorant of the law, and it was this that resulted in the large amount of work for his staff. This campaign was complemented by radio broadcasts and leaflets designed to publicise the law about land management more widely, emphasising the importance of maintaining the agricultural land area. The bureau also conducted investigations in towns and villages in order to assess the scale of violation. The response to a violation depended on the circumstances, we were told. When a case of illegal land possession, by individuals or village, was encountered, those responsible could simply be asked to complete the official forms, thereby legalising the action. This applied particularly to cases where developments that involved illegal land occupancy had brought economic benefits. (It would also protect the local officers in the event of scrutiny from the next tier in the administrative hierarchy.) However, at other times the bureau did take a more punitive approach to transgressors, which sometimes required fines to be paid or the building to be destroyed. Our informant emphasised the lack of cooperation between his organisation and others as a major obstacle to his work. He was referring both to other units within the administrative hierarchy (i.e. county, prefecture, province) and to other units at a similar administrative level, notably the urban construction bureau.

The regulations, at least in general terms, were well understood by Neiguan residents. In our survey nearly 80 per cent of respondents claimed they were aware of the existence of rules forbidding the occupation of cultivated land. Nonetheless, just under half the respondents wanted land for new housing and around 70 per cent thought the town needed to expand further. However, there was a strong feeling amongst our sample of residents that whatever the rules said, good contacts and sufficient money enabled private deals to be made.

The land management bureau was involved in activities other than considering applications for land-use change. They had some finance for new developments in particularly poor areas. An example was the establishment of small orchards. They were also involved in training local farmers in practical work. In addition, and perhaps surprisingly, they also

MANAGING THE LAND

This 43 year-old respondent was the director of the land management bureau of Dingxi county. He rose from the relatively low level of *xiang* leader to his present position partly because of his diligence in Dingxi's terrace construction programme. His presentation of land management issues harks back to an earlier era:

> I feel that the most difficult thing is to implement the land management laws. Though we're basically doing this, problems still remain. This year we've made great efforts to solve them. The first task is always propaganda work - publicising the details of the laws. We target the leaders because without them nothing would happen. We've even paid for subscriptions for them for magazines such as *Land Bulletin*, and we make sure these get delivered to the leaders' offices.

> We also have to carry our propaganda to the masses. This is mainly done through the local radio station and the distribution of pamphlets which provide a clear description of the law. We know that a lot of violations are due simply to ignorance.

> The second thing we have to do is investigate incidents regarding land use and the law. This we do through the 26 *xiang* within the county. We've managed to solve some of the practical problems. In some cases, though people had acted illegally, we made them go through the formal procedures after the event. For example, Youyi village paid more than a million yuan to fill in a reservoir which was state property. This was beyond the law. But after some discussion, we approved their application retrospectively. In fact now the reservoir is a highly productive piece of land which is rented off to various enterprises. The profits meant that Youyi village became an economic success. This year they set up a flour mill. After all, economic development is what it's all about...

served as an intermediary between villages which had a surplus of labour and organisations elsewhere which were seeking to increase their workforce. The director of the land management bureau spoke to us about the attempts to refurbish the large areas of terraced cropland in Dingxi county. There was a spate of terrace building in the 1970s but this ceased following the introduction of the household responsibility system in the early 1980s. Later in the 1980s, terrace construction and repair resumed, but from the early 1990s the amount of such work had fallen again.

Finance for more recent attempts to improve Dingxi's terraced land had been provided partly by a loan from the World Bank and partly from the grain development programme administered by the State Council. During one of our visits, a large group from Yongfeng village was manually engaged in terrace maintenance and repair. Particularly striking was the low ratio of males to females in these gangs because large numbers of males had become migrant labourers. We were told that each household in the village had to provide one person for 20 days each year after the autumn harvest for such work. The aim that year was to complete 150 mu of terrace. This labour was unpaid, although other projects, such as road building provided a very small remuneration of about 10 yuan a day. The terrace building represented a high level of collectivism, although we were assured that its organisation was very difficult, requiring much propaganda beforehand, as well as loudspeakers continually providing encouragement during the labour itself.

Planning

Even before Neiguan's plans for industrial development came into effect, the regulations governing land-use created a kind of *de facto* zoning. A draft plan by members of the China Civil Engineering Design and Research Institute had noted that factories were being located on waste land to the north of Neiguan on either side of the Dinglin Highway, some 700 metres from residential areas. It concluded that this arrangement was 'reasonable' but noted that the bleach powder factory was too close to the town and that polluting glass fibre and flour processing plants encroached on to the main road in the town itself. We found that the local leadership had a reasonable grasp of the principles, particularly the advantages, of zoning. Village leaders conceded that factories located on vacant lots in their villages should ideally be rebuilt by the highway, away from productive land and closer to transport links. The deputy head of Neiguan town, who was in charge of industry, told us:

> We do pay attention to environmental protection. You may be aware that our bleach powder factory once caused a chlorine leakage incident, polluting the crops in the surrounding areas and poisoning pigs at a local farm. That incident is over now, but it was a big lesson for us. Since then, we have begun to closely examine industrial projects. The bleach powder factory is going to be moved downwind of the town in order to reduce the

chances of pollution. Our natural environment is already bad enough, particularly with water shortages, so we cannot make things worse.

Living in Neiguan

Transport and Communications

Each day a coach service passed through Neiguan from Lintao, heading for Linxia, the southern part of Gansu, and further on to Xining and Tibet. In order to join the national rail network, passengers and goods from Neiguan would usually go to the county town first and from there transfer to the Longhai railway. Post and telecommunications facilities had developed rapidly in recent years, centred around the town's post office. There were about 70 lines in the town when we visited.

Housing

Standards of housing varied considerably according to income. In the countryside we found homes built in a farmhouse style which was traditional to the region. Within the town, traditional farmhouses were mixed with newer apartment blocks. The more wealthy residents typically occupied two-storey, brick-built detached houses with a courtyard. Sometimes wood was also used in their construction. The area of such houses was usually around 150 square metres. Slightly less well-off families inhabited brick bungalows. Upper and middle income housing of this sort comprised less than 20 per cent of the town's housing stock. More typically, houses were built of brick and dried mud. They consisted of a central living space and reception area, bedrooms and a courtyard. As farmers became more prosperous they added new rooms and other features. Courtyards varied in size: some were as large as 100 square metres. They were surrounded by mud walls, which some of the more wealthy farmers covered with a large sloping roof and lintels with wood carvings depicting animals and folk myths. The yard itself was usually divided into plots of land for growing flowers and vegetables. Sometimes, pigs or sheep were kept in one corner, often guarded by a dog on a leash. Courtyards were usually built facing south, with the rooms lined up along the northern side. The biggest room, used for dining, relaxing and entertaining guests was in the middle, with bedrooms at either side. The kitchen and storerooms were located at the two far ends of the house. The walls of poorer homes were made from mud and straw. While cheap and simple to build such buildings were nonetheless sturdy and well suited to the dry climate. The roofs of houses were traditionally shaped to maximise the capture of water and to direct it into storage wells. We were informed that the housing stock had improved markedly in recent years. Over 40 per cent of our respondents had lived in their current home for less than 10 years. Some had moved in after getting married, and some had renovated older houses. However, well over a quarter of respondents had lived for over 30 years in unmodernised premises. A minority (14 per cent) had occupied their current house for over 50 years.

House interiors were sparsely furnished. In general we found the furniture to be simple and sturdy. In a typical middle-income family, a large, heatable brick bed (*kang*), covered with a timber frame lay against one wall. Opposite was a cabinet or trunk for clothes. The main feature of a guest room was a metre high altar placed against the north wall where offerings of fruit and food were placed during festivals. In better-off homes, furniture was made from apricot and peach wood imported to the area, but poorer families used furniture made from low quality wood, typically locally produced willow and poplar. We visited many poor families whose homes contained only a *kang* and a few stools. However, the commodification of marriage in China had reached Neiguan. The homes of newlyweds usually contained a colour television set, a sofa, a sewing machine and a wooden bed. Over 90 per cent of surveyed households possessed their own latrines. Members of the other households used public toilets. The public toilets in factories and government offices were poorly maintained and usually extremely dirty due to the shortage of water for flushing. Such places also supported large numbers of flies and maggots.

Fuels

The four-month winter and sub-zero temperatures meant that some form of space heating was essential. Only 17 per cent of households we surveyed depended entirely on coal. Sixty per cent of households used coal in combination with dried crop stems, a traditional fuel which was plentiful and comparatively inexpensive. Coal was used, however, in offices and hotels. Coal was often seen piled up against public buildings. Stoves for heating were also used for boiling water and cooking. Most rooms had a small chimney to remove smoke. All but one of the households we surveyed used electric lights. The single exception was a poor household which relied on an oil lamp.

Waste Disposal

Waste water from industrial and domestic premises was discharged into open channels where it was diluted periodically by rainwater. Most of these channels appeared to be permanently blocked, resulting in a series of ponds from which most of the water either drained or evaporated. However, the quantity of domestic waste water was insufficient to be a significant pollution problem. Some households gave their waste water to their pigs to drink. It was part of the local ethos that water was too precious to be wasted. None of our respondents thought that waste water treatment was necessary. In nearly all the surveyed households human waste from the latrines was collected for agricultural use, so the lack of proper sewerage was yet to be a problem. Many respondents said they also kept uneaten vegetable matter for the same purpose. The quantity and quality of domestic rubbish reflected quite well the stage of economic development of a household or community. All but a few of our respondents had not noticed any change in the composition of their solid waste in recent years. But those who had detected change tended to be well educated, travelled and in senior jobs. Their rubbish contained an increasing amount of packaging and plastic products. Old clothes, shoes and bottles, which would formerly have been recycled, were often now simply discarded. As so little rubbish was generated by most households, there was little understanding of the significance of waste disposal. Very few people knew that elsewhere rubbish was generally taken away and treated. Many respondents said they threw any rubbish into the street or on to the nearest patch of waste ground. Only six respondents said they normally used bins. This confirmed our own observations. We saw that the waste land and ditches around the town contained domestic rubbish, and as previously remarked, the open drain along the '7-5 Road' in the centre of Neiguan's town core area was blocked by litter from nearby restaurants, stallholders, and passers-by. We seldom saw bins in public places, although there were apparently several around the town, and a few full-time street sweepers were employed to collect and remove rubbish. Most local residents we talked to were quite happy with the way waste was handled. These were mainly farmers. Those who were unsatisfied (about 25 per cent) were teachers, office workers and young people - all categories more likely to be better educated than most Neiguan residents.

Food and Drink

The staple foods in Neiguan were wheat, sweet potatoes, ordinary potatoes and millet. Peas and hyacinth beans were also consumed when other foods were in short supply. In our survey 77 per cent of households produced their own grain or were supplied with enough by relatives to meet their needs. Only 10 per cent of surveyed households needed to buy grain from the market, and 12 per cent relied on government relief. The high price of non-staple foods made for a monotonous diet. And many people still had problems securing three meals a day. The poverty and poor diet of some families were striking. Inside the cramped home of one family we visited in Xianfeng village the entire furniture consisted of a bed. The husband was out working on contract but had not sent any money home to his wife and their three young children. After handing over their quota of public grain after the autumn harvest, the family was left with only half a sack of wheat. When we visited, they had little wheat left, although it would be another three months before they would be able to apply again for relief. In Jinping village we visited another poor family and found the mother boiling potatoes. The big ones were for humans, she told us, and the smaller ones for the family pigs.

Vegetable production and local supply had grown rapidly in recent years with the establishment of a vegetable production base and the use of hothouse nurseries. Similarly, improvements in animal husbandry had increased the local supply of pork, chicken, beef and lamb. These developments had generally increased the income of farmers and improved the local diet. One of the main dishes in Neiguan was oatmeal pudding, which was often served with vegetables. Another common foodstuff was *momo*, a kind of pancake made from wheat and millet and which was often served with millet porridge. Local women seemingly prided themselves on being able to make these well. Potatoes, which yield well in the area, took the place of wheat and other grains in times of shortage. The most common vegetables were cabbages, garlic leaves, chillies, radishes and onions. Meat consumption tended to be seasonally confined to Spring Festival. Most farmers kept pigs: the better-off families slaughtered one or two for Spring Festival along with a few chickens and a lamb. Poorer families typically slaughtered one pig, sold half and eat the rest themselves. Those who did not keep pigs would buy pork in the market. Leftover meat was salted, dried, and stored for consumption later in the year. Price was a major constraint on meat consumption, with pork costing about six yuan per jin in the mid-1990s.

For most local residents, eating meat in restaurants was prohibitively expensive. Everyday meat consumption was confined mainly to administrative officials in the town and to a few other town core residents. Fish was a very expensive luxury for Neiguan residents, although it was available in the town's better restaurants. Most of the fish eaten were yellow river carp and catfish. Seafood, however, was virtually unknown. A little food was sometimes consumed between meals. People would occasionally be seen picking the seeds from a sunflower, bought for one yuan in the local market. Other street stalls sold bean jelly, baked sweet potatoes and tangerines, mainly to children on their way home from school. Biscuits and sweets were available in the shops but were not widely or frequently consumed. Children and adults often resorted to chewing a piece of cold *momo* as a snack between meals.

However, people did not appear to stint on alcohol. In slack seasons some people drank quite heavily. Friends were invited to family drinking sessions and the streets often resounded to the shouts of a 'paper-stone-scissors' style drinking game. We met town officials with large appetites for alcohol and saw individuals consuming one or two bottles of spirit in a single session, apparently with no ill-effects.

Tap-water was not available in the town until 1992. Previously, the residents relied entirely on wells and river water. Most work units, and several of the town's residents, had their own wells. A part-time worker in the town's agriculture technology station, told us that as a child the family well was a few metres deep but by 1990 the well had been sunk to over 20 metres in order to reach water. In 1992, the town government improved water supply by channelling river water to the town from a mountain region dozens of kilometres away. The water was now purified for domestic use. However, shortages of pipes, plus a charge of 1,200 yuan (twice the yearly average income), to connect houses to the supply severely restricted access. In our survey only 20 per cent of households had access to tap water. With installation costs four times higher than in Shanghai, the mains-connected households must have been the wealthiest in Neiguan, constituting a kind of 'water elite'. Half the households still relied on wells for their water. In an attempt to increase the availability of potable water the town government set up a dozen or so water supply stations around the town. It was estimated that around 2,000 people made use of this facility. A bucket of water of about 20 litres costed 0.1 yuan at the water stations, which was still a significant sum for middle-income families in the town. One of our guides, whose family were average earners, regularly bought water from the station. Each week, his family of eight consumed just eight buckets of water, a very modest amount.

Education

Just under a fifth of respondents in our survey had no formal schooling, while a further quarter had only attended primary school. A little over a quarter attended low-middle (early secondary) school and the same proportion had attended high-middle (senior secondary school). The middle school in Neiguan took about 1,000 students, with over 300 coming from outside the *zhen*.

Health and Welfare

Neiguan's hospital provided services for people from up to 35 kilometres away, including 13 townships distributed among four counties. Doctors from the County Second Hospital told us there were no epidemic diseases in Neiguan. The hospital director was adamant that claims made by a small number of respondents concerning the incidence of tuberculosis and hepatitis were simply based on misconceptions. We had no means of verifying this statement. There was, however, a serious rodent problem. Over 70 per cent of our respondents had problems with rats in their homes. We saw many dead rats in piles of rubbish or on waste ground. Local residents told us that there were too many rats for the cats which traditionally controlled the rat population. Consequently, there was increasing reliance on poison, although this had also affected the cat population. It was believed locally that the main cause of the rat epidemic was the destruction of vegetation which provided a habitat for snakes, formerly a major predator of rats. Flies and mosquitoes were mentioned as nuisances by nearly 20 per cent of respondents.

Leisure, Customs and Religion

Neiguan's town core served as the centre of culture and entertainment for the surrounding area. There was a library, an 800 seat cinema providing a steady diet of *kung fu* movies from Hong Kong and Taiwan and, importantly, a radio and TV relay station which brought national and international programs. Local *Qinqiang* drama was popular amongst the elderly. Outdoor snooker was a popular pastime for young people. Tables were scattered along the streets, with patrons paying a small amount per game. At fairs and festivals, the cultural diversity of the town became apparent. In general, though, the pace of life here was rather slow and gave the impression that spare time passed slowly, especially in the winter.

Tea drinking was a leisure activity and a cultural form in its own right in Neiguan. *Guanguancha*, or pot-tea, was brewed in clay or enamel vessels, or even old cans, and was heated over an open fire, often in public. People could be seen preparing this in every corner of the town and village. Elderly people were often seen gathering bricks and stones to set up a temporary stove by the side of the street, burning firewood and charcoal, and hanging an empty food can over the fire to boil their tea. This process had been handed down from the days of the Tang and Song dynasties. The tea used was of a plain and robust variety, imported especially for the purpose, and well suited to long boiling.

Over half of our respondents claimed they never read a newspaper. We found that people preferred to get their information from the television or the radio. Most of the sampled households contained a television set, while individuals without a television in their own house said they had ready access to a neighbour's. In fact, watching television had rapidly become a major leisure activity. Almost 40 per cent of our sample said they watched for two hours or more per day, and 60 per cent claimed they were interested in local, provincial or national news.

We found the local people to be direct, honest, and loyal to their local area. And, as we found to our benefit, they also had a highly developed sense of hospitality. In particular, middle-aged and elderly people had a strong sense of place. Most such people were indifferent to the prospect of life in big cities like Shanghai and some were positively averse. Home was the place to be, so long as it provided them with the necessities of life. By contrast, younger people were more critical of their living environment and exhibited a yearning for big city life. Yet they were also apprehensive about being able to adapt to living in a major city.

Three groups of Buddhist temples, the Goddess Palace, *Yaowang* Temple and Temple of Buddha, were situated on the side of Jinjiyuan mountain to the east of the town. These temples were single-storey buildings of very simple structure, and they had recently been renovated using donations provided by local people. Inside were small Buddhist statues and pictures but no other decoration. The temples were very popular with people from Neiguan and neighbouring areas, particularly the elderly, and on holy days they were filled with worshippers.

Future Developments

Neiguan is an official pilot area for small town development and its future direction was a matter of concern for the authorities, right up to provincial level. The aim overall was to present Neiguan as a model of market town urbanisation, acting as an economic focal point for the surrounding countryside as well as setting an example for similar towns in other parts of China. Exhaustive plans had been drawn up covering every aspect of development. These were based on a 50 page planning document produced for the town in 1987 by the China Civil Engineering Northwest Design and Research Institute. The plan envisaged Neiguan as a place of 'rational layout, sufficient infrastructure, prosperous economy, convenient transportation, pleasant environment and strong economic radiance'. The plan envisaged two phases. In the short term, the focus would be on acutely needed infrastructure development, especially transport facilities, running water and electricity. Traders were to be moved from the '7-5 Road' into specialised markets. Much of the old town was to be redeveloped. The local cemetery of revolutionary martyrs was also to be refurbished. In the long term the plan called for the complete reorganisation of the town based on the separation of new industrial and residential areas. Improved sports and leisure facilities were also planned, along with new roads, the development of local beauty spots and an urban afforestation programme. It was envisaged that when all the developments were completed, the town core would cover nearly 3.5 square kilometres. The completion date given for these proposed developments was 2010. However, our own observations together with comments made to us by local officials, suggested this date was somewhat optimistic. The lack of a secure financial base threatened to undermine the proposed changes, and this emanated from Neiguan's lack of resources with which to foster industrial and agricultural developments.

Even comparatively minor developments were constrained by lack of money. There was a plan to install street lighting and renovate a 500 metre section of the main road which passed the front entrance of the town government office. This would have cost an estimated 630,000 yuan. Despite countless discussions with relevant authorities, the money was still unavailable and no progress had been made. One proposal was to seek funding from businesses in Neiguan, but this raised only 100,000 yuan. Another possibility was to request loans from the banks, but there was no real prospect of servicing the debt. Despite these constraints the head of

Dingxi county's environmental protection bureau maintained his optimism:

> Neiguan's infrastructure was very inadequate and dated. Now, the official plan for the place has been compiled and has proved to be practicable. The upgrading of two roads in the town would get support from township enterprises. The provincial construction committee has also pledged 20,000 yuan for setting up a market. It was better to get the projects started as soon as possible. Once they are under construction, it becomes easier to apply for more funds. The China Agricultural Bank and Construction Bank have both set up a credit fund and hopefully we will get access to it. Everyone is thinking about developing profitable businesses.

It remains to be seen whether this optimistic view of Neiguan's future is well founded.

Note

1. Traditionally, China is divided physiographically into three realms - Eastern Monsoon China, North-west Arid China and the Qinghai-Xizang Plateau. Each realm is divided into Natural Divisions, which in turn are divided into Natural Regions.

3   Yuantan

Location and History

Yuantan *zhen* is situated in the south-west of Anhui province in the lower middle reaches of the Yangzi river valley. Administratively, Yuantan is part of the city of Anqing which lies on the northern shore of the Yangzi about 50 kilometres to the south-east. The northern part of the lake of Caizi hu, which is directly connected to the Yangzi, is situated approximately 50 kilometres to the east. Hefei, the provincial capital, is about 175 kilometers to the north-east. The county town Qianshan is 24 kilometres to the north-east. The border between Qianshan and Tongcheng county is provided by the Dashahe river which flows to the east of Yuantan. Qiban and Sanmiao counties lie to the south; Chashui and Longguan counties lie to the north, and Lingtou is to the west. The town is a road transport hub, the site of the intersection of the Beijing-Zhuhai and Shanghai-Nielamu national highways (national road numbers 105 and 318). Smaller roads connect the town with remote areas of Qianshan county and a network of village roads has been built to connect outlying settlements with the town.

Yuantan has a long history, dating back to the Han dynasty (202 BC-220 AD). It was formerly known as Yuantan Pu, but that name was changed to Yuantan town in the middle period of the Ming dynasty (1368-1644). More recently, the Guomindang made Yuantan a prefectural centre, responsible for the administration of nearby towns and settlements. In the 1950s, under communism, Yuantan prefecture was placed under a regional government. This format was replaced by the People's Commune system in 1958. The Yuantan People's Commune governed four administrative districts comprising 18 production brigades and 113 production teams. In 1961, the commune was again replaced by a Yuantan regional government which had the town under its direct jurisdiction. A set of changes in 1992 abolished the regional tier of government and merged Yuantan and Shuangfeng prefectures. From 1994 onwards the Yuantan prefecture assumed control of the town itself and of 18 outlying villages, six being situated in the mountains.

Physical Environment

Yuantan is situated on the Dashahe and Lutanhe rivers which flow into Caizi lake to the east via the local Red Flag reservoir. The town core and part of the town's agricultural area is located on flat land typical of the Middle and Lower Chang Jiang Plain Natural Region. This forms a sub-zone of the Humid Subtropical Division, which is itself part of the Eastern Monsoon Realm (see note on Page 60). However, part of the area under the town's jurisdiction encompasses the lower foothills of the Dabieshan Mountain range which lies to the north-west. Huoshan mountain (1774 metres) is about 50 kilometres away, while the national park of Tianzhushan mountain is somewhat closer.

The Lower Chang Jiang Plain Region comprises a soil geographical subregion of the cambisol soil region of China (Zhao Songqiao, 1986). Soil types are predominantly eutric gleysols, characterised by a humus content of about three per cent near the surface, a high water table and impeded drainage. The north-western part of Yuantan *zhen*, however, is much more characteristic of the Tongbi-Dabie subregion of the Dabie-Micang Mountain Region. In this area, a complex mosaic of soil types occurs due to variations in parent materials, relief, topography and land-use history.

Climatically, Yuantan lies within the humid subtropical monsoon zone. There are four distinct seasons; winters are cool and summers are hot and wet. The climate of Hefei, which is located some 175 kilometres to the north-east, is representative of the lower lying part of the *zhen* and serves as an appropriate reference (Zhang Jiacheng and Lin Zhiguang, 1992). January is the coldest month with a mean temperature of around 2ºC. However, the incursion of cold air can lower temperatures well below zero. Mean July temperatures are around 28ºC. Between May and September mean monthly temperatures exceed 20ºC. Mean annual rainfall is close to 1400 millimetres, over half of which falls between April and August. On average there are some 250 frost-free days per year, although somewhat fewer in the more hilly parts of the *zhen*.

The potential vegetation of the area is either broad-leaved evergreen forest or mixed forest (Zhao Songqiao, 1986). The uncultivated land in the hills was now covered for the most part by coniferous trees, chiefly species of pine (*Pinus*). The comparatively young age of the trees was due to a reforestation programme initiated in 1979 following large-scale felling during the years of Great Leap Forward (1958-1961). At the time of our visits, some 30,000 mu of hilly land had been planted with trees. Stands of bamboo had also been established in the hills, partly in an attempt to revive the manufacture of traditional local crafts. The *zhen* contained some 10,000 mu of intensively cropped land on the plains. Yuantan is criss-crossed by a network of streams and pools, which often served as nodes for village development. Water was provided for everyday use and villagers had also developed commercial aquaculture, including fish, water chestnuts and lotus roots.

Yuantan's Appearance

Yuantan's urban core was surrounded by an area of countryside which contained 18 villages. The town centre occupied approximately 15 hectares while the whole *zhen* covered 96 square kilometres. The urban area contained administrative offices, factories and other enterprises, warehouses, extensive retail outlets, schools, hospitals, a power station, a cinema, and residences. There were indications that the prevailing level of economic development was stretching the town's infrastructural capacity. For example, on our last visit a much-heralded piped-water project had yet to be completed, street lighting was inadequate and public hygiene facilities were extremely poor. Telecommunication facilities were also inadequate for the surge in demand that had recently occurred. Moreover, the highway network, so influential in Yuantan's development, had fostered extensive and haphazard ribbon development. Factories, markets, restaurants and shops were scattered in a disorderly way by the roadside. This raised the amount and cost of infrastructure necessary and made rational planning more difficult. The town had a somewhat chaotic appearance, with different forms of land-use mixed randomly together, and narrow twisting side streets adorned with clusters of electrical cables. There was much to be done to resolve such problems before imposing more ambitious schemes.

Administration

The elected members of Yuantan's people's congress were subject to the ratification of the people's congress in Qianshan, the county town. Further up the administrative hierarchy was the city of Hefei, the capital of Anhui province. The Yuantan people's congress, which consisted of 85 deputies, met twice a year, in March and September. Its chairman told us his three major duties were planning the town's construction, its economic development, and its educational facilities. However, he believed the people's congress should have had wider responsibilities, citing the investigation of poverty which was so clearly prevalent in the outlying hill villages. He also felt the people's congress should act as a conduit for residents' opinions concerning the government's policy and its implementation. The chairman of the people's congress also attended the Yuantan Party committee, but had no voting rights.

The nine members of Yuantan's Party central committee was led by the Party secretary. There were four deputy secretaries and the other members were, respectively, the head of the discipline inspection committee, the head of the military department, the deputy head of the town, and a member of the organisation committee. One of the deputy Party secretaries also served as Yuantan's town head. He had four deputies and three assistants, two of whom had special responsibility for the villages in the hilly parts of the *zhen*. In addition, the town government maintained offices for administration, economic management, political and legal affairs, urban construction and household registration. The standing committee of the people's congress of Yuantan appeared to us to be somewhat moribund. There was a chairman of the standing committee, but not, apparently, a committee to chair. The same applied to the local branch of the people's consultative conference. Although this organisation had a liaison officer it was not clear to us what duties were implied. There were no branches of either the official workers' or farmers' unions in Yuantan. The women's federation and a youth league were represented, and each had a full time chairperson. In addition to the administrative personnel, Yuantan had a range of executive staff attached to state-owned industries. These personnel were responsible for the local application of national development policies in areas such as banking and financial services, utilities management, policing, education and health, communications and media, and agriculture. The affairs of Yuantan were thus run by a tightly woven coterie of public institutions, with the Communist Party at its heart.

The tax structure at town and prefecture level dated essentially from 1984. Locally, tax was the object of scorn, being known as the 'revenue for meals'. It was considered a good year when tax revenue covered the wages of township staff. The problem lay in the continued weakness of Yuantan's economy: although the local economy had developed rapidly since 1990, it had done so from a very low base. This was reflected in the per capita annual income from tax. In 1995 the value was 80 yuan, 20 yuan less than the county average. We found that the tax situation pressed heavily on the minds of local officials: indeed, the intricacies and inconsistencies inherent in taxation seemed to be their favourite topic of conversation. The town itself could not levy taxes autonomously, and had to pass on a proportion of its revenues to the county government, effectively making it a tax gathering arm of the county. Three quarters of the tax revenue came from industrial and commercial levies. Because of the shortfall from such sources, infrastructural projects relied on money raised from the public, which the town was encouraging under the slogan 'the people's town built by the people's money'.

In 1994, the town leadership initiated a wide-ranging investment programme in public facilities. One million yuan was made available from public funds. In addition, a drive for private contributions from Yuantan expatriates was instigated. Unfortunately, the money raised was insufficient to meet the costs of the new sewerage system, the public toilets and the side-walks planned for the town. As a result, the focus had shifted to establishing revenue generating projects as a means of financing the public works programme.

Demographic Aspects

Frequent changes to the administrative boundaries of Yuantan made it difficult to estimate changes in the size of Yuantan's population. Accordingly we provide the trends in the years before and after the designation of Yuantan as a town in 1991. The Yuantan Region Annals record a population increase from 29,100 in 1949 to 59,700 in 1987. The periods of greatest absolute growth were 1949-1957 and 1962-1975. An increase in mortality in the aftermath of the Great Leap Forward caused the population to stagnate between 1958 and the early 1960s. Since 1981 national birth control policies had been more strenuously implemented, with a consequent decline in the rate of population growth. In 1992, the year after its designation as a town, Yuantan's population was just over 31,000. Since then the population had steadily increased: we were told that if the floating population was included, it was around 50,000 by the mid-1990s.

In our survey, 49 per cent of households contained four or five persons, 21 per cent contained six or more individuals, and 30 per cent of households contained three or fewer persons. Mean household number was 4.3. Only six of our sample of 133 households had more than eight members, and three of these households were on the point of division. These data belie the general perception of large household size in rural and small town China. Most of the households encountered during the survey were *zhugan* families, consisting of one young or middle-aged couple, one or two senior citizens and one or two children. This indicates a co-existence of traditional, extended families and modern, nuclear families, but a noticeable trend towards the latter.

The low number of children per household indicated how effective the state family planning policy had been in this area, notwithstanding historical rural traditions. Nonetheless, above quota births did occur. Furthermore, many of the people who had emigrated to find work gave birth to their children elsewhere and returned to register them in Yuantan, a situation that birth control officers could not prevent. In rural areas, couples simply kept trying for a son, no matter how many daughters they may produce in the intervening period. In response, the authorities conducted random household inspections. Women with above quota pregnancies were pressured to have abortions, and families with excess children were fined. Although these measures were difficult to undertake and to enforce, the birth control team had managed to maintain their quota of births. One of our visits coincided with family planning month. The building in which we stayed in Qianshan, the government guest house, was the headquarters for the officials who were conducting the work in the surrounding area. Each day they would leave early for the countryside and return in the evening when there was a communal debriefing session. There was clearly unease on the part of the officials because of the presence of outsiders who would like to have quizzed them about their work. We were informed that the work team was actively coercing individuals, with occasional punitive action, such as the destruction of houses, against transgressors.

As elsewhere, the household registration system was implemented after the promulgation of the PRC household registration guidelines in 1958. The system separated urban and rural residents, and in the early days, the local people fell into the latter category. The people's commune was the registration authority while the production brigades reported births, deaths and migration monthly to the commune. The information was collated at the end of each year to provide information on local population trends. Although the administrative system in Yuantan had changed, household monitoring remained essentially the same. For example, new-born babies in the town had to be registered at the household management office, receiving either urban or rural designation. To facilitate data collection, rural households had to report once a year to the town, while urban households had to do so once every two months. Registration procedures for death and migration were similar for urban and rural residents. In the past, the effect of the rural-urban distinction had been to give people a fixed position from birth. Rural residents could change their status only through education, by marriage, or by military service. This system made the management of migration relatively straightforward. According to local officials, marriage remained the main cause of migration: mostly it took place between people in the same household registration category and who lived within the same county. The data for the period following the designation of Yuantan in 1992 clearly showed that immigration from other provinces was far lower than that from other places within Anhui.

Despite the seeming rigour of data collection, a growing discrepancy between the formal system and reality was evident. Throughout China, agricultural reform and the demand for cheap labour from the towns and cities had resulted in increasing numbers of people, particularly the younger men, moving from rural areas in search of work. Yuantan was no exception. According to the town government's estimate, in the mid-1990s around 3,000 Yuantan people, or about a fifth of the town's labour force, were working or doing business in China's major cities. Favoured destinations were Nanjing, Guangzhou, Beijing, Shanghai, Tianjin, Qingdao and Dalian. Some men had succeeded in moving their entire families to their destination cities. Migration conformed to a pattern, with migrants often returning to their home village to help with the harvests and for Spring Festival, but going back to the cities for most of the intervening periods. Not all the migrants were unskilled or semi-skilled labourers: a significant group consisted of commercial travellers representing the township enterprises. Qingtian village alone employed over 200 people in the sale and marketing of the village's brush products. Migrant workers could not register as urban residents in the cities where they worked; nor, officially, could they move their families from the countryside.

The advantages and disadvantages of large scale migration from countryside to city are well known in China. While creating certain problems for the destination cities, a large influx of migrants provides a ready pool of labour for urban construction and for the service trades. For the migrant's home town and family there is a tangible benefit in terms of the wages earned and remitted, and of course migration eases the surplus rural labour problem. However, there may also be problems for the families left at home. During our investigation, we found that many households were in effect headed by a young to middle-aged wife who had to take care of a child, or children, and often both sets of parents as well. She would also have responsibility for the contracted farmland. Moreover, these women felt under pressure from neighbours and relatives to perform the conventional social role of women in rural China. As well as enduring physical and mental pressure, such women often expressed anxieties about their husbands - not only their welfare but also the temptations they faced in a big city. The social aspects of migration are complex, but have certainly constituted a force for change in contemporary China. For example, migration has tended to erode the traditional distinction between city and countryside, and returning migrant workers serve as vectors for ideas and values gathered in the large cities.

We were told that younger people who had gone away to work had returned to Yuantan with unsavoury habits. A school teacher told us:

> There are many people here who go to other places to work and it is a good thing for them to broaden their horizons and increase their incomes. But problems have also been created. Most of our emigrant workers want to make money and improve their families' living conditions, but some young girls have fallen, dazzled by the world outside. Also, people are now so busy making money that their children are left uncared for, which is not healthy. Many children are left to their grandparents who tend to spoil them.

We saw evidence of this in some of the households we visited. For many people the focus of life had shifted from their families to their businesses. And while business has boomed the home had frequently become a somewhat desolate place, inhabited only by a child with his or her mother, or even grandmother, for company. One household we visited consisted of a mother and her two children. Her husband was away working and she only saw him for one month a year. No other family members were in evidence and it was apparent from simply looking at the children that they were lonely and neglected. We understood this to be a growing phenomenon.

As well as out-migration, there had also been movement into Yuantan. According to the director of the town's Party and government administrative office, new arrivals were usually either business travellers with temporary registration permits, transients stopping off on their journey along the highway, or farmers from the surrounding countryside who had managed to change their registration status. Since 1984, when national *hukou* regulations were changed, Yuantan's town leaders had allowed farmers to settle in the town if they came to work permanently or set up businesses. Some 700 people had taken advantage of this provision by the time of our visit. The township head told us that these newcomers had to meet three conditions. They had to demonstrate that they had secured gainful employment, that they would make a financial contribution towards the town's development, and that they would come off the grain 'dole' that supplied the population in emergencies. The majority of these new townspeople had taken work in local factories or in the construction industry. The financial requirement was originally set at 3,000 yuan, but was later halved to encourage in-migration. Although ostensibly a contribution towards the town's building costs, many of our respondents simply regarded their payment as a straight swap - cash for urban registration. The third requirement was intended to keep welfare costs down as the town grew and was the only difference in entitlement between old and new residents. With the establishment of open grain markets and floating grain prices, this requirement had become virtually meaningless by the mid-1990s. There was also a transient population in Yuantan, registered at local hostelries and liable to random inspection by the local public security bureau. Those seeking accommodation needed a personal identification certificate, and had to declare both their reasons for visiting and the length of time they intended to stay.

The increase in the migrant population exacerbated the problems of enforcing birth control and household registration policies. Among migrants, we were told, births tended to be more frequent than officially permitted. The authorities responded by refusing settlement rights and fining offenders. Household registration officers told us that the increasing number of migrants made it hard to obtain information. Deaths were rarely reported, they said, because newly arrived visitors had no appreciation of the importance of household management and the population census.

Income and Work

The Yuantan Annals recorded major changes in income and living conditions for local people since 1950. Superimposed upon a directional trend of increased prosperity were fluctuations, caused usually by changes in central policy. Prior to the establishment of the PRC, over 90 per cent of Yuantan's workforce was engaged in agriculture, and the area was said to be struggling to maintain food self-reliance. The situation improved somewhat between 1949 and 1957, during which time the government oversaw the land reform, collectivisation, and the establishment of the People's Communes in 1958. The state's emphasis was very much on supporting agriculture. Poor households also benefitted from government relief. Following the disastrous aftermath of the Great Leap Forward, in the period 1963-1965, under the readjustment policy 'adjustment, consolidation, enrichment' the burdens on farmers were reduced as quotas were set locally to reflect actual conditions. The local economy was thus able to recover somewhat. However, the Cultural Revolution (1966-1976) disrupted the economy once more and conditions did not improve significantly until the introduction of economic reforms in the late 1970s. During the 1960s, before the reform period, some township enterprises were established in Yuantan, albeit in embryonic form. State policy at this time determined that commune and brigade level industrial activities should be geared towards agriculture and that the scale of such enterprises should remain comparatively small. Even so, this added a new dimension to rural existence. A minority was able to gain experience of factory work, and just a glimpse of urban lifestyles. Local leaders realised that agriculture and industry were not necessarily incompatible. The unofficial slogan prior to the Cultural Revolution was: 'Grow food for yourself on the farm, make money for yourself in the factory.' In the post-1978 period, increasing numbers of rural labourers turned to the off-farm sector for work, a trend which was promoted by government policy. During the 1980s and 1990s industrial and agricultural production had grown significantly and the personal wealth of many of Yuantan's resident had increased. However, it was clear that this increased prosperity had not been shared evenly among town residents.

One feature of recent economic development in China has been the involvement of public officials and institutions in private enterprise. For example, during our interview with the head of Yuantan's agricultural machinery station, we learned that he ran a bone processing factory in his basement. Apparently it was thriving at the time because a shortage of the product had brought about an increase in price. He now employed seven workers and clearly took some delight at being the boss and not working himself.

Officially, just over half of Yuantan's labour force worked on the land in 1994-95, which compares with over 90 per cent in the pre-reform era. Nearly 60 per cent of our respondents described themselves as peasants. A further 20 per cent were either cadres or professionals. Around 40 per cent of respondents, particularly the peasants, had second jobs,

---

YUANTAN'S DEPUTY PARTY SECRETARY

This respondent was the 56 year-old chairman of the Yuantan People's Congress. From 1960 until 1978 he was in the People's Liberation Army in the eastern province of Zhejiang.

Being demobbed from the army and coming back to my hometown, I was conscious of two changes: firstly, in the army it's all plain speaking and a commanding attitude. But in local government affairs you've got to adopt a different method - things are more complicated and if you don't do so there'll be trouble. Secondly, it was 1978 when I came back to Yuantan - just the year the reform started. Before, the countryside was a closed shop, and everything came down with the state's plan and nothing was allowed except farm work. For example, one Party secretary from Chang'an village lost his job because he encouraged people to take up courtyard production - meaning the planting of fruit trees. He also said people could go off and do building work. Such things were officially the 'capitalist tail' and had to be wiped out. So the policies prior to the 11th Party Committee meeting in 1978 kept the countryside poor. In Yuantan nearly all the buildings were simple and single-storey. After 1978, policies were relaxed and everything got better in the countryside. Restrictions were eased and compulsory planning was reduced step by step. Now many families live in two-storey buildings. From closed to open, from poverty to prosperity - these are good policies.

---

mainly in industry, commerce and household handicrafts. We talked for instance to one family whose lives were devoted to making small sculptures from local bamboo, and an elderly man whose beancurd was highly regarded locally. Interestingly, despite the fact that the vast majority of his earnings came from his sideline, he insisted that he was a farmer. For those who had not taken second jobs or started sideline businesses the reason cited was usually lack of opportunity rather than disinclination.

According to the director of the town office, the annual average income in 1993 for township factory workers was 2,000-2,500 yuan, for workers in transport and communications it was 5,000 yuan, while other service sector employees earned around 3,000 yuan annually. In the same year, the average per capita income in Yuantan was 450 yuan. Given the wide variety of different occupations, businesses and trades that were practised within single households, or even by individuals within those households, family economics were clearly complex. It was apparent to us, however, that the wealthiest families in Yuantan were those which focused on the most profitable forms of non-farming activity. Those tied to unprofitable labour on the land were trapped outside the wage economy, thus making it impossible to raise the capital, or find the time, to develop viable schemes for sideline production.

The modal income range for households in our survey was 5000-7000 yuan. Just under half the respondent households, and 70 per cent of respondents, received no regular wage income. All but a few households earned at least some money from agricultural sideline production, from as little as 50 yuan to as much as 8,000 yuan annually. Eighteen of the households we surveyed earned up to 12,000 yuan annually from handicrafts, from renting property or various other activities. Our wealthiest respondents were those whose main occupation was running a retail or manufacturing business. Fifty-seven per cent of our respondents rated their income level as satisfactory while 42 per cent claimed it was unsatisfactory. When asked what they intended to do about their income dissatisfaction, those with definite plans overwhelmingly favoured going into trade. Very few people thought that farming gave them any opportunity for economic advancement.

Disparities in income between households posed major problem for the town's administration. Over 7,000 people endured the harsh conditions of six mountain villages. In such areas there was widespread and acute poverty, with a per capita annual income of around 200 yuan. The town government spent 80,000 yuan per year on supplies of relief grain for these villages because they produced, on average, only half the amount required. We repeatedly heard the view that the best hope for such villages was in diversifying and specialising, perhaps in tea production, mulberry trees, medicinal herbs, fish farming or forestry. One problem, however, was that few of these enterprises would bring a quick return, so it was very difficult to secure the necessary investment. Banks, we were frequently told, did not lend to those without a firm financial foundation. Nonetheless, the 80,000 yuan annual grain subsidy for these villages could perhaps have been better spent in developing sustainable, and ultimately profitable types of agriculture and other enterprises in this difficult hill environment.

While problems were most acute among farmers in the hilly parts of the *zhen*, according to the chair of Yuantan's people congress it was also hard for farmers on the plain to raise sufficient crops on the amount of land available to them. But instead of relinquishing their contracted land, the farmers clung all the harder to them, or at least a small part of them, as an insurance. The yield from the better quality land in the *zhen* was reputedly good, but input costs, for fertiliser, pesticide and equipment, were high, and increasing. The situation was exacerbated by the quota system which forced farmers to sell goods to the state at a lower price than could be achieved on the open market. The situation worsened in 1994 when the state removed subsidies on diesel and fertiliser and stopped paying farmers in advance for grain quotas. With prices from the state declining and production costs increasing, more grain was being channelled to the market. However this increase in supply tended to depress prices. As a result, many farmers were operating at a loss. Rather than drive farmers out of business, however, it simply reinforced their dependence on home grown supplies.

Sharp contrasts in living conditions were evident throughout Yuantan, within the town core area, between villages, and within villages. Some villages, like Qingtian, tended to be prosperous, in fact very prosperous, in comparison with the mountain villages. Within the same village some households struggled to feed themselves while the annual income in others was apparently in excess of 10,000 yuan. We visited both kinds of families. The former possessed virtually no furniture or other materials. The latter, in contrast, usually had a big front garden and the house had modern equipment and conveniences. We were told that families in such extreme wealth or poverty were in a small minority, yet both extremes were highly visible.

Agriculture

The *zhen*'s plain contained some 10,000 mu of intensively cropped land. The most important crops were rice, wheat and oil-seed rape. The long growing season permitted two to three harvests a year. Traditionally, the farmers brought in two harvests a year, wheat and oil-seed rape in summer, and paddy rice in autumn, but this pattern began to change in the 1950s with the introduction of double cropping of rice. This change had increased agricultural output markedly. Ninety per cent of local rice land was now double cropped. Other factors which had contributed to a growth in production were increased use of fertilisers, pesticides, irrigation, the introduction of new varieties, and a limited degree of mechanisation. We observed farmers burning rice straw in the field after the harvest. This local practice was designed to replenish soil minerals. Farmers occupying sloping land had begun to develop cash cropping and animal husbandry. Part of the hill land was terraced for grain production and some producers specialised in the production of Chinese medicinal plants. There was an increasing trend to grow mulberry (for silk worms) in the hill villages. Vegetables were grown widely on small, privately owned plots whose size varied according to the number of family members. The vegetables were used primarily for personal use, although occasionally surplus products were sold in the market to provide a little cash income. In addition, five 'vegetable bases', or market gardens, with a total area of 100 mu, had been established around the town. Buffaloes and oxen were kept on farms for draft purposes while pigs and cattle were raised for meat. Rabbits and pheasants were also raised.

The pattern of farm work was dictated by crop growth cycles, with peaks of activity concentrated in summer and autumn when rice was planted and harvested and winter crops of oil-seed rape and wheat were sown. The work was heavily labour intensive and during these seasons many migrant labourers, and town employees, returned to their family farms to help. (We found during our summer visits that some local factories had suspended operation for this reason.) The amount of labour available was believed to be a key factor in determining the size of the harvest. At other times of the year, the burden of labour often fell on women of working age. Several of them complained strongly to us that they had to look after their families and tend the land while their husbands were away doing contract labour.

Mechanisation was still very limited on farms in Yuantan. This was due, first, to the cost of most machines being too high for individual households, while groups of households had not yet devised practical ways of sharing the costs between them. Second, the scattered plots assigned to families under the household responsibility system were too small to make mechanisation a practical proposition. A change in this fragmented management system seemed to be a prerequisite for the adoption of even a limited degree of mechanisation. Decollectivisation was nonetheless widely acknowledged to be the chief factor responsible for breaking the vicious circle of rural poverty.

Yuantan's natural resource base had greatly diversified during the reform period. The former forest cover was almost completely stripped during the Great Leap Forward (1958-1961) and reforestation began in earnest only during the 1980s. Because of the long production cycle the main economic benefits of tree planting were yet to be realised, although lower branches were legally removed for firewood. There were other benefits of restoring tree cover, particularly the reduction of soil erosion. Since the implementation, in 1981, of the 'three designations' (*sanding*) policy (i.e. establishing ownership, marking the boundaries and defining the responsibility system for hill land), forest farms had flourished. These enterprises, which were developed by villages, or federations of households, ranged in size from around 100 mu to over 1,000 mu. Our impression was that farmers had taken to them with enthusiasm. The production of bamboo, which was put to many different uses, had also been officially promoted and we saw many stands in the hilly parts of the *zhen*. Bamboo was the most conspicuous item for sale in the booths that line the important highways in the area. The local government had became closely involved with the structural adjustment of the agricultural economy, taking market forces as the guiding principle, and an increase in farm household income as the objective. This was part of a more general drive to increase the number of cash crops grown in an attempt to reduce the town's dependence on grain production. By the mid-1990s, the town was harvesting tea leaves, silk cocoons and a variety of fruits in significant quantities. Sideline production of this sort was generally called 'multiple undertakings' or the 'garden economy'. In the years prior to reform, and under their previous name of 'capitalist tails', such activities were banned. The cultivation of mulberry trees was particularly important in the hill areas where the yield of conventional agricultural crops was low. Sanhe village had expanded its mulberry fields year by year from the end of the 1970s. Over half of the 300 households in the village were now involved in mulberry growing and sericulture, producing 10 tonnes of silk cocoons annually. Yuantan people had also diversified into medicinal herbs, animal husbandry and fish farming. Pig and poultry farming had developed very markedly. By the mid-1990s the town had an average of three pigs and 20 poultry birds per household. Some farmers had benefited greatly from diversification. A farmer in Guanghui village, told us that he had a 100 mu peach farm yielding over 7,000 kilograms of peaches a year, which earned him an income of over 10,000 yuan. The director of the town's industrial office commented:

> I am considering setting up an agricultural enterprise, maybe a vegetable farming business. I once raised this with the authorities. Most of our vegetables come from Anqing and Qianshan county town and I think this is a weak point in our local economy. In addition there is also a need for more multiple undertakings like fruit production. We must develop big agriculture (*da nongye*).

In summary, since 1980 Yuantan's agricultural economy had diversified considerably, a process which had brought individual and collective benefits. Farmers had seen their incomes increase and many had been able to generate the cash necessary to expand their activities. The commercial base of local agriculture has been widened and the growing market for produce had maintained agriculture's importance in the town's economy. Nonetheless, it was also clear that developments in agriculture were insufficient to sustain economic growth of the town: such growth was reliant on off-farm activities.

Industry and Commerce

We were assured repeatedly that Yuantan entered a new, and rapid, phase of development after the key Party plenary of 1978 which set the post-Mao reform in train. This applied particularly to the off-farm sector, though as previously mentioned, some activities developed during the 1960s, primarily to serve the needs of agriculture. By the mid-1990s there was a variety of non-agricultural enterprises in Yuantan, including a range of service and manufacturing establishments. The scale of the latter varied, from household to industrial level. The town also had warehousing facilities for grain, cooperative storage facilities and wholesale depots. Several dozen state-owned trading houses coexisted with over 100 private businesses, including 20 restaurants, hairdressers, photography studios and other small-scale service establishments. The town's industrial-scale activities included the production of plywood, tyres and plastics. The town's construction industry was also well developed.

While township enterprises in Yuantan remained relatively backward when compared with the highly developed coastal regions, the economic basis of the town had been transformed since the beginning of the reform era when agriculture provided 95 per cent of total output value. In 1979, there were just 58 township enterprises in Yuantan, with an annual output value of about 1.5 million yuan. Progress was very rapid in the 1980s and by 1987 the number of township enterprises had risen to over 1,000, with an aggregate output value of over 25 million yuan. After its re-designation in 1992, Yuantan town's administrative area was much reduced, but the number of township enterprises within its jurisdiction continued to grow. The annual output value was now in excess of 300 million yuan, while the average annual growth rate remained in excess of 50 per cent until the mid-1990s. By contrast, agricultural output managed only four per cent growth annually in the same interval. Clearly, township

CHAIRMAN OF YUANTAN PEOPLE'S POLITICAL CONSULTATIVE COMMITTEE

The respondent joined the Party shortly after Liberation, but his landlord family background made him a regular target of political movements. He is now also involved in business.

I'm 59 years old and I come from Qipan *xiang*, near Yuantan. My great-grandfather was the youngest in his family and he decided to study. He built a house which was the best in the village. My father inherited the property but not the traditions of study; he went into business. My uncle was a finance director for the county under the Guomindang and it as this that brought all the misfortune. In 1949 I was studying at middle school when the land reform teams were being recruited. To my surprise I passed the exam and became a team member at the tender age of 14 years. A couple of years later I joined the army, and got into the Party in 1956.

I was a young man without much experience. The only thing I could do was to follow the leaders and copy articles out for them, as they were illiterate. I also had to write their documents for them. But because of my family background I couldn't be made a leader myself.

The Cultural Revolution came as a big shock. I was sent off to do reform through labour, and then to Wanghe village to be an ordinary secretary. In 1976 I was recalled to Yuantan and the county Party committee asked me to be the head of a *xiang*. I said I would only be Party secretary of a *xiang* because being a head was just a nominal post. So I stayed in my job as a junior secretary, even though lots of my colleagues were promoted even up to the county level, despite the fact that their education was nothing compared with mine. Finally in 1990, the upper levels gave me a choice - either to be a deputy Party secretary or to be the People's Political Consultative Conference chief for the whole of Yuantan. I chose the latter, and I now combine it with a bit of property development for myself.

continued...

industry had become the main engine of growth for the town.

Our field work in the mid-1990s revealed 2,248 township enterprises in Yuantan. Forty-five of these were run by the town, 103 by villages, but the great majority - about 2000 in total - were organised either

In fact the Consultative Committee is pretty toothless although our six members in Yuantan want to do something for the area. So I made four suggestions. Firstly, we should try to tap our own resources by sending teams to cities where Yuantan people have migrated. We should get them to contribute to their home town in terms of capital, technology and information. Secondly, we should go out and discover the positive experiences of others. For example, a lot of the petty traders in Yuantan come from Yiwu in Zhejiang and Changshu in Jiangsu. Their money doesn't stay in Yuantan. But it shouldn't be difficult to produce these goods here for ourselves. It would be easy to copy the fashions of Hong Kong or Thailand and make and sell clothing here. Thirdly, we should develop the property market. This will also help good planning of the town. Fourthly, I think we should develop the tourist trade. Yuantan is the 'base camp' for Qianshan and it's the east gate of the Tianzhu mountains.

From my point of view, cadres at town and village level are pretty poor. Their work is mainly thinking up ways of getting more money or grain from the people and to oversee family planning. The former Party secretary was transferred because his attitude was bad - he only looked after himself. We don't have meetings here to promote development. The central government holds two main meetings about agriculture each year but in Yuantan there seems to be no planning for its development. The relationship between the cadres and the masses is a tense one. The key to this is to develop the enterprises and strengthen the collective economy, so the burden of the peasants is reduced. At the moment some of the enterprise leaders are mainly concerned with enriching themselves. I think rural enterprises should remain collectively owned, while commerce can be done privately.

by household cooperatives or private individuals. Of the total number of enterprises, 60 per cent were engaged in labour intensive light industry, 30 per cent were construction companies, and 10 per cent were involved in various types of trade and commerce, including transport and retailing.

There was no heavy industry in Yuantan. A number of enterprises produced construction materials including plywood, bricks and prefabricated concrete. These accounted for about 30 per cent of those engaged in township industries. The chemical sector was represented by plastics, fertilisers, fireworks and iron-sand. The iron-sand was extracted locally from waterways and was used to produce magnetic materials. Other enterprises were involved with packaging, food processing and light engineering, particularly machine parts. One local village had developed a very successful brush making enterprise.

We heard that 80 per cent of Yuantan's non-agricultural output was sold within Anhui province, particularly within Qianshan county. Magnetic materials and paint brushes were sold into a much wider market, including the south-east coastal regions, Hong Kong and South Korea. Industrial brushes had even penetrated the United States. In terms of output value the contribution of the town and village-run enterprises was similar to that of all the cooperatives, including household cooperatives, in the *zhen*. The town and village-run enterprises, although only a small part of all Yuantan's off-farm activities provided the town with most of its revenue. As a result they received more attention - and investment - from the town authorities. The head of the town told us: 'We prefer to provide assistance to the key enterprises run by the town. Only big enterprises like these are able to provide large sums of revenue.' Enterprises to have benefited from this investment policy included those involved in the manufacture of magnetic materials, plywood, plastic products, aluminium and steel window frames.

The magnetic materials factory provided a good example of an enterprise whose development had been steered by the town's investment policy. When originally set up in 1985, this enterprise was simply a purchasing company for iron-sand. In 1992 it collaborated with a regional mining research institute and invested three million yuan in new technology. Then the enterprise became involved in the manufacture of electronic components. In 1994 a further tranche of six million yuan was invested to build finished magnetic products. In another major investment 1.2 million yuan was made available to a plywood factory to upgrade its production line. Its diverse range of products was marketed throughout eastern and central China. Large investments of this sort came mainly as loans from the People's Bank of China, the Construction Bank and other state finance houses. Ninety per cent of this money went to designated key township enterprises. By the mid-1990s the output value of 14 town-run enterprises accounted for half that of all enterprises in the *zhen*. Each of these 14 enterprises had an annual output value in excess of 1.1 million yuan, and six of them were in excess of three million yuan. We also found signs of more sophisticated market opening measures, including two joint stock companies, which had issued shares worth nearly four million yuan. Two other projects relied on foreign investments. A 'Taiwan Mansion' had been built with three quarters of a million yuan invested by a Taiwanese

---

DIRECTOR OF YUANTAN'S INDUSTRY OFFICE

This 54 year-old cadre held a key position.

I graduated from junior middle school and for my first job I was a projectionist in the local cinema. Later I was sent to the Electric Power College in the capital, Hefei. After working in a couple of *xiang*, I came back to Yuantan in 1992. When I was in Shuangfeng *xiang* back in 1985, I started to get involved in off-farm enterprises. I was a secretary in the *xiang*'s offices. My nephew went to work in a neighbouring county and fell in love with the daughter of a household that had a private brush making business. They married and returned to Shuangfeng *xiang* in Yuantan. They decided to use the woman's brush-making skills and start up a business on their own, so they came to me to borrow funds. I found the boss of a *xiang* credit cooperative who happened to have been my schoolmate, and he lent me 400 yuan. My nephew and his wife each got their hands on more money, and eventually they had capital of 3-4,000 yuan. From the beginning they did well, and soon they built a new building costing 17,000 yuan. My eldest son then wanted to have a go. I sent him to Anqing for training, and on his return we set up our own little factory. Now 24 of the 29 households in the village have their own brush making businesses. Some are big (up to 80,000 yuan in output value a year) while some are small (20-30,000 yuan). At first the sales were limited, mainly to Sichuan. Later they were extended to Fujian, Guangdong, Jiangsu and Zhejiang.

Some of the young people aren't satisfied with just making brushes. Seven or eight of them got together and set up a brick works. There's a good market. The next step is to build a stone crushing plant for a cement producer.

---

entrepreneur whose family origins were in Yuantan. The other project, the Yuan Company, in which a Singaporean partner has placed half the equity, was a joint venture to manufacture electronic components.

Yuantan's cooperatives, many of which were located in the countryside, accounted for half the town's industrial output. In the several villages we visited most of the local cooperatives started from a single household or several households with family ties. These were referred to as 'individual businesses' and 'household cooperatives' respectively. Such businesses began, typically, with an investment of labour and skills in the collection and development of local resources, for example, iron-sand, bamboo and hog bristles. Some of these enterprises had developed into mature household industrial and commercial concerns which attracted a certain amount of capital, and fund growth from their own resources. The epithet 'specialised' was attached to some villages because of the way their off-farm activities were concentrated in particular areas. Qingtian village, known locally as a specialised brush-making village, was a case in point. Here, over 80 per cent of households had set up businesses producing hand-made bristle brushes.

At the outset, brush making was limited to the production of ordinary paint brushes for sale within Anhui province. The profits from these enterprises were invested in new technology enabling the village to produce a wide range of industrial brushes, including those used in precision instruments. The market had expanded from Anhui to Fujian, Guangdong, Jiangsu, Zhejiang and Sichuan provinces. Villagers were planning to invest still more money and market their brushes internationally. The development of brush making had completely changed Qingtian village. By 1994, per capita income had reached 1,500 yuan, which was around three times the town average and certainly more than all the other villages in the *zhen*. Half the village families owned motorcycles and many lived in newly built houses. Inside such houses it was typical to find a range of white goods and consumer electronics. We were told that the living standards had already reached the 'national affluent' standard and that Qingtian had become the 'affluent model village' for Yuantan *zhen*.

The rapid development of township enterprises had not only brought a growth of income for local people, but also increased the economic strength of the town. Importantly, tax income had increased substantially due largely to the development of township enterprises. Between 1990 and 1995, for example, tax revenues increased by a half. Industry and commerce accounted for around 80 per cent of the total, while agriculture and forestry made up the remainder. By encouraging investment in its key enterprises the town leadership was both securing revenue for itself and income for local people.

While the economy of Yuantan had changed markedly in the reform period, problems still remained in the off-farm sector. Certainly, the plywood factory, the magnetic materials factory and a handful of other factory enterprises had been successful, but the majority of enterprises were not really profitable, and some were on the brink of closure. Another issue was the policy of 'loans to the rich not the poor'. Although the availability of credit, principally from the banks, for township enterprises, household cooperatives and private businesses, had been a key feature in promoting Yuantan's economic development, there were widespread grievances about lending policy. Loans tended to go to those businesses whose profitability had already been demonstrated while those enterprises which needed investment to become profitable were denied the loans necessary to update their equipment. As a result they were left to make low value products.

Practically all our respondents felt that further development of township enterprises was necessary in Yuantan. And over 85 per cent were optimistic that living standards would continue to improve. Economic optimism ran high in Yuantan and this seemed to be linked with the progress of township enterprises. Also, we found that the desire for further industrialisation and urbanisation was higher in this town than in the other two towns we studied, possibly because of the large number of inhabitants who have travelled to, or have worked in, the developed cities of the coastal region.

Anhui people have a reputation in China for being adept as traders and commercial operators. For many years following the establishment of the People's Republic this was not a heritage to boast about. And even in the early years of economic reform, a distaste for commerce still lingered on in government policies and practices. We were told of one incident in the early years of reform concerning a visit by the head of a county security bureau from Guangdong province. After finishing his official business, he went to the county town and set up a stall selling clothes he had brought from the south. Local security officials smelled corruption and arrested him under suspicion that his identification was forged (surely no self respecting cadre would hawk clothes by the roadside). After telephoning Guangdong they were told that it was standard practice among 'southerners' to combine official trips with private business. This came as something of a shock to Yuantan residents, but it alerted them to the shifting economic reality of the early reform period, and also we might surmise, awakened latent entrepreneurial instincts. As township enterprises developed in response to government policy, they were complemented by a spontaneous growth in small service businesses such as shops, restaurants, market trading, and transport.

Around 200 traders came daily to Yuantan's town core to hawk their wares from the roadside. Most were from the nearby countryside, but a few travelled from the mountainous parts of the area. During winter we bought charcoal from a mountain villager who had produced it himself (unfortunately the charcoal was of poor quality, badly prepared and it emitted more smoke than heat). Official market developments in Yuantan had had mixed fortunes. The town construction department built a market in the mid-1990s for local farmers. It was well planned, and in accordance with government regulations on traffic management it was situated away from major roads. However, the market was ignored by local farmers who preferred to ply their wares by the roadside opposite the market gates. It was here that local residents were used to doing business, while the passenger vehicles and inter-provincial truckers provided local traders with a steady flow of customers. In contrast, the new Chaoyangmen small commodity market, opened in January 1994, had been much more successful. Funding for this market, which cost over 600,000 yuan, was raised from private traders. Daily turnover when we visited was reported to be almost 100,000 yuan. It consisted of several wide avenues of two-storey buildings. The shops, which were situated on the ground floor, sold a wide variety of daily necessities, clothing, shoes, fancy goods and consumer electrical equipment. The upper stories provided living accommodation and storage space. This format had proved successful enough to attract business from nearby towns and customers from neighbouring counties. In fact, since the late 1980s Yuantan had become the main trading centre for the local region.

Certainly, we usually found the market bustling with trade. All 70 shop units were occupied. The goods were brought in from various places in China, and in some cases from abroad. In addition, four specialised markets catered for the trade in construction materials, agricultural produce, general commodities and bristle brushes. Apart from the shops in Chaoyangmen market, there were dozens of outlets along the main road. Most belonged to the County Trade and Marketing Cooperative but displayed none of the bad habits traditionally associated with state-owned retailers. A combination of reform in the state cooperative system and an excellent location for business had helped integrate them into the market. As the retail sector had grown, so too had associated services, especially restaurants, transport, communications and banking.

The 20 or so restaurants within the built-up area of the town were mostly privately run and specialised in cheap simple meals, often based on rice or rice porridge. Snacks were on offer from mobile food stalls. Numerous guest houses along the main traffic route provided both accommodation and meals. We visited a small restaurant run by a 60 year-old couple who grew their own rice and vegetables and bought their meat from the market. The work was hard, they said, but their cooking was good

DIRECTOR OF THE GENERAL OFFICE FOR INDUSTRY AND COMMERCE

A former accountant in a county office, this 32 year-old man occupies a key position in *zhen* management in Yuantan.

There are eight people in the bureau. We're responsible for the following: ideological work, business registration and licensing, enterprise management, market research, contracts, advertising and trade marks. We report to the county's equivalent bureau. We're very concerned with the stability and order of the market. The fees we charge for the above services are mostly ploughed back: for instance, we set up the Chaoyangmen market in Yuantan.

We gather fees from every market stall, and management fees on top of this from each trader. But because the market isn't near the town centre, sales are small. Originally we charged 10 yuan to each stall per month. Later many shifted to the roadside to avoid these fees and we now get them to pay a two per cent tax on sales. This usually amounts to about six yuan per stall - they mostly sell local farm products as well as handicrafts.

We have to deal with pressures both from collective enterprise management and from the growing private sector. Our investigation work is difficult. We have to deal with a lot of breaching of contracts and flouting of trade marks. The market is awash with pirated alcohol and cigarettes. I can resolve a case where the penalty stands at less than 200 yuan or if illicit funds of under 1,000 yuan are confiscated. Other cases have to go up to the economic investigation department of the county bureau. Yuantan Salted Foods factory turned out products such as prawn crackers with 'Made in Shanghai' on their labels. They were stopped from doing this and were fined 1,000 yuan.

At present we have a total of 394 regulations at our disposal. Last year the higher levels made us get rid of around 100 more. We feel that national edicts such as the Trade Marks Law, or the Regulations on the Development of Enterprises and Management of Registration are often insufficient or inappropriate. So we tend to make up our own detailed rules.

and the business was thriving. A conspicuous phenomenon in this locality was the rapid growth of combined petrol stations and restaurants to service the increase in long-distance traffic. The location of Yuantan on the intersection of major east-west and north-south highways had ensured that the number of vehicles, particularly long distance trucks, passing through the town had increased very considerably recently, and no doubt would continue to do so in the future. When driving at night it soon became apparent that most such enterprises engaged young women whose initial task was to approach (often very dangerously), and flag down vehicles. It appeared that these young women also acted as hostesses, and straight forward prostitutes. As the principal targets for their attention were long distance vehicles, this development could have serious public health implications. We witnessed the flagging down of one long-distance truck travelling from *zhen*jiang on the south coast to the northern port of Qingdao, with a load of bananas. The young woman negotiated a 'package' of accommodation, food and services with the driver and his mate.

During our fieldwork we met several people who had voluntarily left work in township enterprises or gave up opportunities to work as migrants elsewhere - both previously the summit of rural aspirations - in order to set up their own service businesses. It is reasonable to predict that the growth of the service sector will be a major feature of Yuantan's future development.

Before reform, banking services were provided by a sub-branch of the Agricultural Bank and a small credit cooperative. Subsequently, the financial sector had grown in tandem with the local economy: the two most opulent buildings in town, built in the early 1990s, were branches of the state-run Construction and Industrial Banks. These new banks seemed to signify that Yuantan was moving towards a fully-fledged commodity economy, even though other sectors of the economy, and public services particularly, remained poorly developed.

Environmental Issues

Natural Hazards

Yuantan is not subject to major life-threatening natural phenomena, although water issues do pose temporary problems. During times of excess rainfall and high river levels, serious flooding occurred which could lead to significant reductions in crop yield. We were told that this problem was exacerbated by the loss of tree cover in the hilly parts of the *zhen* during the 1960s. It is certainly logical to expect that the loss of woody vegetation would increase both the amount and the rate of water discharge from the hills. The gradual restoration of a forest cover, which we remarked on earlier, should improve this situation in the future. However, the hill areas are also subject to periodic drought during the summer months. Town officials told us that the repair of water conservancy facilities was a priority because after decollectivisation maintenance had been inadequate.

Pollution

We were unable to obtain biophysical data on air and water quality locally, and have therefore relied on the responses of residents during the survey, information provided by key informants and our own observations. Between 75 and 85 percent of respondents rated air quality as 'fresh' or 'very fresh', and the taste of water as 'good' or 'very good'. These findings corroborated our own general assessment. However, 26 per cent of respondents felt the taste of their water had changed in recent years, which could reflect increased pollution loads. The proportion who claimed that a deterioration in air quality had occurred was only 16 per cent. Nearly a quarter of respondents rated their local area as 'quiet' or 'very quiet', but 30 per cent felt noise levels had increased in recent years. Fewer than 10 per cent of respondents were aware of pollution incidents locally.

Land Loss

The familiar phenomenon of agricultural land loss to housing and industrial development was conspicuous in Yuantan. We could not find official data for land transfers out of agriculture but unofficially it was well known locally that the rush to set up small industrial zones after 1992 precipitated a considerable loss of cropland. It was estimated that by 1994 around 1,000 mu of arable land were claimed for this purpose. The annual loss of arable land had probably been around 300 mu throughout the 1990s. The authorities, we were told, had strengthened control on land management in order to preserve cropland. Officially, industrial projects were submitted at the planning stage to the county planning committee. If approved, the project moved on to the land bureau, the environmental protection bureau and the urban construction bureau of the county government for further consideration. If the proposed development was to occupy less than 3 mu, the county land management bureau made the final decision. Otherwise, the application went up to the provincial land bureau. Compensation was exacted for land taken from the present occupier. At the time of our visit the price was around 30,000 yuan per mu, of which 20,000 yuan was the cost of the land, 3,000-4,000 yuan compensated for the value of the crops, and the remainder was used for labour force reallocation.

Although regulations were in place to control agricultural land ioss it was clear that there were difficulties in their implementation at local level. We interviewed two local officers involved in this process in Yuantan. One of our informants was the Party secretary of Yuantan's land administration bureau. He was essentially a party worker, drafted in to his present position without previous direct experience of land issues. We were not impressed by his grasp of environmental matters in general, although he did emphasise the importance of minimising land loss. Before the introduction of land-use regulations, land was transferred out of agriculture quite freely, but this had now changed. An office of land management was established in Yuantan in 1987, with a staff of three. In 1991 the office was split into two; one section became the current land administration bureau while the other became the urban construction planning bureau. Our informant told us that anyone wanting to build on cultivable land had to submit an application to the land administration bureau. However, there were considerable difficulties in enforcing the regulations: often, individuals would simply build on cultivable land without prior permission, or else the amount taken out of cultivation would exceed the allowed amount. In response, the bureau sometimes pulled down buildings, which led to local ill feeling and agitation, and sometimes required the involvement of the courts. The work of the land administration bureau was not confined to implementing land regulations, but included afforestation, the development of courtyard economies, and issues which impinged on public health, such as encouraging the separation of working and living areas in buildings. The bureau raised money by way of a land tax, which was passed on to the county. Seventy per cent of the bureau's income came from public sources, but they had to find the remainder themselves. Some of these funds were apparently used for reclaiming waste land. The bureau had a staff of 25, which our informant believed was inadequate.

Since 1991, when the land management office was split in two, there had also been a branch of the county level construction planning bureau in Yuantan. Our second main informant on land issues, one of a staff of two in this bureau, was responsible for planning in the town core and in the surrounding rural area. He was only 23 years old, and had graduated from Anqing's 'professional construction' middle school, where he specialised in planning, just three years previously. He told us that his office's main remit was to 'create conditions for economic development', and he was clearly quite proud of what the office had achieved during a time of considerably enhanced economic activity. He cited the new shopping complex in the town core, tree planting along the town's highways, and a major reforestation scheme in the hilly areas of the *zhen* as examples of his work. He emphasised that his attempts to effect change relied heavily on cooperation with the local government, and also the village communities. All this, he said, required appropriate propaganda. Every development, whether a new house in a village or a modification to a building in the town core should, in theory, first be approved by the town construction and planning office. He described the regulations as 'very strict', citing the case of a household which had been made to destroy an extension to their own property because it was erected without the necessary permission. In general he felt his office enjoyed good cooperation with other official departments in the town, which was apparently not the case in many other towns he knew. Nonetheless, there was clearly a limit to the power of the planning department in influencing the town's development. For example, they wished to site enterprises in such a way as to minimise their impact on the town and its residents, and to optimise resource use. However, he complained that such concepts were alien to many cadres, and indeed to the town government. Accordingly, new developments had gone ahead without reference to the planning department until the building was underway, and then economic imperatives prohibited any intervention. Our informant was in favour of zoning; for example, siting polluting enterprises downwind of residential areas, and clustering smaller enterprises close to the market where the goods would be traded.

While Yuantan's planning office had the state's comprehensive set of regulations at its command, and various other county level documents containing planning guidelines, the reality on the ground was that Qianshan was a poor county, so poor in fact that in some months the officers received no salary. It is not difficult to appreciate why good practice was not always adhered to. Despite professing good cooperation with other administrative sections in the town, our informant expressed his concern about the lack of coordination between his own office and the land management bureau regarding the building of new houses. In theory, each application should go first to Yuantan's construction planning office, which then made the necessary amendments before submitting it to the land management bureau. But in practice many applications were sent directly to the land management bureau, who often gave their approval. However, the planning office did have the ultimate sanction and our informant cited cases of new buildings or extensions being pulled down and their occupiers fined. What particularly annoyed him was the fact that the land management bureau was fully aware of the correct procedures, but still chose to act unilaterally, probably because of financial gain. He believed the best way forward was to combine the activities of the two departments, as had happened in some large cities.

The salary for the two staff in the town's construction planning office - just 3000 yuan a year in the mid 1990s - was generated. until 1994, by a management fee imposed on persons who were engaged in new building projects. However, in response to appeals from the farming community concerning the unreasonable burdens imposed by these fees, they were abolished. Not only did this mean that the staff could not always be paid, it also meant that their promotional work was severely curtailed and they could not do the investigative work in the country areas which was felt to be so important.

Living in Yuantan

Transport and Communications

The first major road through Yuantan was not built until 1929. A number of new roads were built in the 1950s and laid the foundations for excellent road links with other parts of China. The town was located at the intersection of the Beijing-Zhuhai and Shanghai-Nielamu national highways (national road numbers 105 and 318). Smaller roads connected the town with remote areas of Qianshan county while a network of tractor trails connected Yuantan's town core with its surrounding villages. Nonetheless it was only in the late 1990s that certain of Yuantan's villages were being opened up to motor transport. Good roads and regular bus services connected Yuantan to the county town of Qianshan. The railway was 20 kilometres away, at Gaohe. Anqing, about 55 kilometres away on the Yangzi, had had an airport since 1994. From here there were flights to Shanghai, 45 minutes away. Anqing, as a significant port on the Yangzi has long been connected by boat to other towns and cities along the river.

Locationally, therefore, Yuantan was very well placed to take advantage of the new economic opportunities available in the reform era.

The growing numbers of people coming to buy and sell in Yuantan had led to a boom in the private transportation of people and goods. These utilised a wide range of motor vehicles, including tractors. We visited one such business run by a father and his two sons. They had originally bought a four tonne goods vehicle to carry raw materials for township enterprises. Having made some money with this work they started a passenger transport business which provided a daily minibus service between Yuantan and Qianshan, the county town. These (*zhongba*) services successfully plugged a major gap in public transport provision. The vehicles were usually bought second-hand from a city, where typically they had failed inspections, were patched up and set to work. General business growth since the 1980s had raised the demand for post and telecommunications. Most local businesses were connected to IDD and DDD land lines, and cellphones and pager networks were becoming increasingly common. Courier services were also available and widely used.

Housing

Housing construction had speeded up in the 1990s, reflecting the town's economic development and population growth. The town leadership had recently tightened its rules against using cropland for housing construction, much to the frustration of local people in both the town core and the countryside. The conflicting demands for housing and agricultural land were making it hard to 'live and work in peace and contentment', which was the sentiment expressed in so many of the calligraphy pieces that adorned the walls of local residences. Housing in the town core and the nearby country districts consisted predominantly of two-storey buildings, and older single-storey dwellings. The former had generally been built since the mid-1980s and were constructed mainly of brick, timber and concrete. The ground floor in these relatively simple dwellings usually comprised a sitting room, kitchen, toilet, and a store-room. Upstairs there were usually three bedrooms. There was a small front yard, often used for growing flowers or vegetables. The single-storey housing was built of black bricks and tiles. Such dwellings were most common in the older parts of town, and often appeared rather shabby and dilapidated. The buildings were typically planned around a frontage of three central south-facing rooms, with two more rooms abutting the ends and pointing north.

These two rooms were used for sleeping and often formed the side wings of a small courtyard. The main room of the house, known as the central room, was used for dining and receiving guests. Entrance was by means of an impressive double door while much of the floor space was occupied by a large square table surrounded by four benches. Framed family pictures were hung on the wall directly facing the door, with pride of place going to deceased parents. In many houses these were accompanied by brush pictures and calligraphy on the traditional themes of long life, good health and prosperity. The spaces next to these were often occupied by pictures of film and pop stars from Hong Kong and Taiwan. The room to the east of the central room was used as a kitchen and contained a range, a big water vat, a long wooden table where bowls and plates were placed, and several stacks of firewood or straw for cooking. Under the sloping roofs, families lived in a cosy, even stuffy environment, amidst characteristic aromas of earth and woodsmoke. The courtyard was typically cemented over and used to dry clothes, grain and firewood. At the back was a toilet, a one metre square outhouse containing either a bucket or a pit. In the countryside the yard was usually much bigger and typically adjoined fields, which could be privately owned or allotted under the responsibility system.

When wealthier families built new houses, they preferred to use the same land, gradually razing their old property and building an improved version around the original kitchen. New houses could be distinguished by often elaborate decorative tiling in various colours. A brick wall was usually built to enclose the front yard and finished with solid iron grillwork gates through which newly acquired motorcycles could often be seen. In addition to the privately-owned houses, there was also public housing in the town. This was owned by work-units and attached to government offices and state-owned institutions. Such housing, usually of one or two storeys, was provided mainly for the use of officials working away from their families. Entitlement to public accommodation depended on position, seniority and availability. Rents were very low and often paid by the employer as a perk.

Fuels

Electricity came to Yuantan in 1964 and initially was principally used for farm machinery. Over 30 years later it had expanded to the extent that it played a vital role in households as well as greatly facilitating economic growth. Hydroelectric power stations have been built nearby. Supplies were sufficient for the needs of both industrial and domestic users, the township enterprises being the biggest consumers. Residential demand was rapidly increasing with the greater use of electrical consumer goods, particularly in the town-core area. We were told that power cuts were officially a phenomenon of the past, although personal experience led us to think otherwise: a dinner party for us, hosted by the local leaders, was in the event taken by candlelight. All the households in our survey were supplied with electricity, although we did visit some private dwellings in the more rural parts of the *zhen* which had none. Wood was the predominant fuel type among around half the surveyed households but bottled gas was used by about 10 per cent of households and was apparently gaining in popularity. Gas was too expensive for residents on average incomes. Many households and workplace canteens used coal-dust briquettes. Even the households which used electricity and gas still relied largely on traditional materials such as firewood or rice straw for fuel. Firewood was very commonly used in the hilly regions of the *zhen*. The use of charcoal, mainly locally produced, was generally confined to mid-winter. The consumption of diesel and petrol was increasing as the number of personal and commercial vehicles rose while some of the local factories used specialised fuels such as heavy oil.

Waste Disposal

Traditional waste disposal practices were the norm in Yuantan. Ninety per cent of the surveyed households used earth closet lavatories while the remainder resorted to public lavatories. In most households the domestic waste was used to fertilise the land. Only two households had waste-water plumbing in their house. Just 11 per cent of sampled households used bins for rubbish disposal. In fact there was no official waste treatment or disposal system in Yuantan. Nor could we detect a demand for improved waste management services: nearly all respondents were quite happy with the prevailing arrangements. Nonetheless the direct disposal of untreated waste was a certain cause of pollution, with public health implications. The fact that over 85 per cent of our respondents had problems with mouse or rat infestations suggested that better methods of waste disposal were an urgent priority for Yuantan.

Food and Drink

The staple food, and main local crop, was rice. Nearly 90 per cent of respondents had their own grain supply, while the remaining few relied on the market or the public grain supply. Rice was usually steamed for lunch and dinner and served as porridge for breakfast together with home-made pickles of radish and mustard. Pickles were prepared by cutting the plants into strips and drying them in the sun before mixing with salt and chili and sealing them in a clay pot. They would be ready to eat after a week or so and would keep for several weeks. The amount of non-staple food eaten, mainly vegetables and meat, varied with income. Some people in urban Yuantan grew vegetables in the front or back yard to supplement their diet. In the countryside nearly everybody relied on home-grown produce, apart from some residents of the mountain villages where land was most scarce. Not having to buy vegetables was in fact considered a perk of farming, although people did come to town to buy produce which was not grown locally. Nearly 90 per cent of our respondents kept animals of some sort, including many in town-core locations. Pigs were raised for sale, although typically a pig was slaughtered at home to celebrate the Chinese New Year.

Fruit, drinks - alcoholic and otherwise - cigarettes and snacks were all widely available from restaurants and market stalls. Some apples and bananas were eaten, but generally fruit consumption seemed low due to its high price. In the town-core area people consumed large quantities of sweets, cakes and other snack food. Tea drinking was ubiquitous. The local officials we met always seemed to carry their own supplies with them when they travelled to outlying villages. Many stalls in the town offered noodles, dumplings, pancakes and other hot snacks. In general Yuantan people eat a traditional diet, although economic growth and altered lifestyles had brought opportunities for some dietary innovation. Almost 75 per cent of surveyed households obtained water from wells while most of the remainder used pond or stream water. Naturally occurring water was still considered to be potable locally, particularly in the hill regions. Only one household in the survey had piped water.

Education

A major constraint on the town's development was the lack of a skilled and educated workforce. Moreover there were insufficient resources to train people to the required level. According to the 1982 population census, 55 per cent of local people above primary school age were illiterate or semi-literate, only four per cent had a high school education and just 0.1 per cent had been educated to degree level. We do not have official statistics for the 1990s but according to the headmaster of Yuantan Middle School, between 50 and 60 per cent of primary school children progressed to middle school. Due to shortages in education funding, schools were generally poorly staffed and not able to meet educational targets. Indeed it was difficult to meet the statutory requirement for nine years schooling. In our sample of Yuantan residents about 20 per cent had received no formal education and a further 38 per cent had attended primary school only. Twenty-three per cent and 11 per cent respectively had been to lower middle and higher middle school, while just five per cent had attended college or university. The general lack of formal education was evident too in the town's leadership: in the local authority, only the newly appointed township head had been to college. The chairman of Yuantan's people's congress emphasised to us the need for better management for the township industries in order for the town to develop further economically. Because of the poor educational profile of the local population, a high school diploma seemed to be an immediate passport to a managerial post. At the magnetic materials factory, the most technologically advanced of the local enterprises, the manager, himself a high school graduate, told us that half his staff were educated to the same level as himself while the rest were middle school graduates. As part of its upgrading process the factory was planning to employ some young and highly qualified staff to undertake professional training. But investing in intelligence was risky, the manager told us, as he could not be sure that these people would stay after their training. He believed that the way forward was to make the enterprise itself more attractive to qualified people by raising salaries, offering welfare benefits and improving the working environment. In the plywood factory, most of the workers had only a lower middle school or primary education.

Similar problems affected the hospitals, schools and other specialist organisations in the town. And there was also a shortage of skilled labourers and craftsmen. We met a few such people when they returned home for the New Year festival. When we asked why they did not stay and contribute to the development of their home town, they all replied that they were not needed. The opportunities for work and high wages in the cities of adjacent Jiangsu province acted as a powerful incentive for skilled labourers in Yuantan as elsewhere in China. The township head told us: 'All our attempts at developing township enterprises here encounter the problems of poor educational qualifications and out of date ideas. Places like ours have not had a successful model to follow.'

Despite this generally low level of educational achievement, the facilities that did exist were of relatively high quality and were founded on a local tradition of respect for scholars and scholarship. The main educational institution was the Yuantan high school, which offered both middle and high school diplomas. Children were fed into the school through a network of local primary schools, but in addition the school attracted fee-paying students from other areas. The deputy headmaster told us something of the school's history and its present situation. The school was set up in 1959, and initially was principally concerned with vocational training for agriculture. Over the years it developed sufficiently to offer a high school education. The school had 46 teaching staff in the mid-1990s, mostly trained in provincial-level colleges, and over 1,000 students. Since 1990 the school had enrolled above-quota students (i.e. from outside the district), at a rate of about 70-80 a year. The fees were around 1,600 yuan per year. The school also opened classes for those intending to retake the national exam for universities, and charged each candidate between 200 and 300 yuan. We were assured that the proportion of graduates from the high school going on to universities was the third highest in the county, and some individuals had achieved very high scores. It seemed the school enjoyed a very good reputation, so much so in fact that some students came from Anqing city, some 55 kilometres away. We were told that school fees were invested in the school: recent developments had included a laboratory block, a new teaching block, a new canteen and toilets, and improvements to the sports field. The income from students retaking their university entrance examinations went towards staff bonuses. When we visited, staff monthly income was around 500 yuan, which was above average. We were assured that teachers at the school were happy to concentrate on teaching instead of looking for a second job. We cannot verify this, but certainly it has been a very common practice for teachers in China to supplement their relatively poor incomes with other work. The high school budget was assigned from the county education bureau, although administratively it was controlled by the town. Other secondary schools in the town were funded from a variety of sources, including the township, an education tax from farmers, and donations from the public and from township enterprises.

In the early days of economic reform, many families wanted their children to help them make money. Increasing personal wealth, it seems, had brought with it a new attitude towards education. Primary school education in the town had been developed to the point where it was universally available, and, in theory, compulsory. Parents who did not send their children to school could be punished. The town intended to extend this practice to middle school in the future. However, few farmers' children progressed to high school: as few as two from each village was typical according to one estimate we heard. Moreover, less than 20 per cent of all junior middle school graduates in the town went on to senior middle school.

There were rewards for those who graduated from high school. We were told that high school graduates had the pick of local employment opportunities, moving straight into management posts in township enterprises in some cases. Others had set up businesses, with a significantly higher success rate than those less well qualified. Yet despite the clear benefits of education, the high school in Yuantan was increasingly experiencing disciplinary problems, reflecting changes in society at large and the fact that many fee paying students were badly behaved and academically listless. The high school deputy head was, of course, anxious to assure us that the problem was under control. The school also suffered from the problems faced almost everywhere in China's educational system, namely lack of funding and low pay for teachers. One of the teachers told us:

> Having worked as a school teacher for dozens of years, I am deeply aware of the importance and difficulties of education. But we teachers only receive a meagre salary of 300 yuan a month. Youths in their twenties working in the bank start on 800 yuan. I have to teach during the day and mark homework and prepare lessons for the next day in the evenings, and in addition I have a plot of land to look after. Sometimes I am very unhappy with the situation. Young teachers are more outspoken and complain that they are stuck in the job. No wonder there is a shortage of teachers.

This perspective captured a nationwide problem, and one which was particularly prominent in poorer rural areas, or where there were plenty of opportunities for more lucrative employment.

Health and Welfare

There was one public hospital in Yuantan, and its 68 staff members served the entire region. We were told that all the doctors came from the region and they were assigned to the clinic on graduation from medical school.

Technologically, the hospital was capable of all the normal surgical procedures including cancer operations, and even kidney transplants. A second, larger, hospital was under construction, apparently as a response to the floods which devastated Anhui in 1991. The World Health Organisation had provided half the 500,000 yuan cost of the new hospital, the remainder came from the town and county level governments. The plan was for the old hospital to be converted into residences. The new hospital was intended to provide improved standards of care, although very specialised work would still need to be done elsewhere. The head of the hospital told us that the cancer rate was very high in the town, with stomach cancers being particularly common. Another major cause of fatality was heart disease. Epidemic diseases, however, seldom occurred, apparently due to widespread immunisation programmes, and perhaps because Yuantan was a national test site for health education. Vaccines were stored at the hospital for collection by small clinics based in the outlying villages, where an ongoing education campaign had convinced people of their effectiveness. Measles, polio and encephalitis had almost been eradicated from the area. When a serious outbreak of meningitis occurred in Qianshan county in the early 1990s, Yuantan remained unaffected. Thyroid deficiencies, once very common in the mountain villages, had been much reduced after the villages were persuaded to add iodine to their cooking salt.

Despite considerable progress, serious problems remained in health-care delivery, particularly to poor people. We met a family consisting of a widow and her two school-age children. The widow's husband, the family breadwinner, had died a year ago. When he was taken ill the family lost its income, and medical charges had left them badly in debt after his death. The widow had suffered a stroke and was unable to work. The family land was looked after by neighbours and relatives but the family itself had no income, leaving the woman in a very distressed state about feeding her children and paying their school fees. Rural families in China show great resilience after floods and droughts, but many have been crushed by medical bills. While urban residents still enjoyed free health care for the most part, this had ended in the countryside with the introduction of the household responsibility system. The well equipped new hospital will have no impact on the many local farmers and their families because they will not be able to afford to use its facilities. We were told that rising medical costs had caused some local people to turn to bogus practitioners, fake drugs and even witchcraft.

Public Security

Information on local crime and other public order issues was provided, somewhat guardedly, by the head of Yuantan's police station. His parents were peasants and he had been educated to middle school level before going to Anhui Public Security School for two years. After five years as a 'people's policeman' in Huangbai, he was transferred to Yuantan. Yuantan's police station reported directly to the county level public security bureau. Four police officers worked in the station and four others were out on patrol. Their salaries were between 3,500 and 5,000 yuan per annum. The number of officers, we were told, was not sufficient given the town's area and the number of villages under its jurisdiction. This problem was exacerbated by poor material resources: the police station was located in a 'temporarily borrowed' house, and they had at their disposal only four telephones, two bicycles and three motorcycles. Nonetheless, the head of the station was convinced the situation in Yuantan's station was better than in many other towns in the region. The two greatest problems for the police were disputes between ordinary citizens and the presence of a large number of migrants in the town, i.e. the 'floating population'. The latter was another consequence of the town's location at the intersection of two important national highways. Our informant felt that some Yuantan residents who had gone elsewhere to work returned with 'bad social habits', although the nature of these was not elaborated upon.

The police were assisted in their work by village-level security protection committees and conciliation committees, the latter being run directly by the court. Each village security protection committee was supposed to meet on a bi-monthly basis to resolve what we assumed to be comparatively minor issues. They called in Yuantan's police officers only if disputes were not settled at the local level. If the case was too serious for Yuantan's station it was referred to the county, which had its own system of patrols. Although Yuantan's police station was directly controlled by the county-level station, it was also accountable to the town government and the Party committee. We learnt that neither interfered in law and order work, but the police were involved in particular issues which resulted from central government policy. Our informant cited family planning and land allocation as two such issues. For example, they were involved in fining (and perhaps punishing in other ways) those who transgressed national laws concerning the number of children. However it was abundantly clear that it was not always easy to catch those who transgressed in Yuantan.

Leisure, Customs and Religion

We were told that Yuantan's first black and white television set arrived in 1976. In our survey, 90 per cent of households possessed a set, although only just over half the households had a radio. The director of Yuantan's government office told us that about 400 households in the town had cable television. The favourite television programmes were the news, films, and soap operas, in that order. Sixty-three per cent of respondents claimed to watch up to two hours daily, but a further 30 per cent claimed to watch more than two hours, in some cases up to six hours daily. Given the low level of literacy locally, the television - and to a lesser extent the radio - was probably the major source of information about the outside world for the majority of Yuantan people. For some it was a leisure activity in its own right. A little under half the respondents claimed to read magazines or newspapers on a regular basis. Such reading material consisted of local and national newspapers and magazines. Illiteracy probably accounted for this comparatively low figure. Socialising with friends and, particularly among the older men, playing mah-jong, were common leisure activities.

Organised leisure facilities were few in Yuantan. The main attraction was the single (300 seat) cinema, which showed Chinese-made films one or two months after they finished their run in the big cities and which were attended overwhelmingly by young people. Yet Yuantan did have a cultural centre, the decline of which illustrates how radically the town had changed. Its director informed us that the centre was built in 1979 with 13,000 yuan provided by Anqing municipal cultural bureau. It was his task to bring to local people those cultural activities - painting, calligraphy, folk dancing and opera - which were consistent with the Party's idea of 'a good time'. He assured us that when it was built it was the best building in town, although it was now among the most dilapidated. He rather regretted the neglect of cultural work during the economic developments of the reform period. The cultural centre had only two full-time employees: former staff had left to work in other government posts or to start their own businesses. Staff members had little work to do. Their most important duties, it seemed, were to produce a work plan at the start of the year and a summary at the year end. In fact the director had so much time on his hands that he attached himself to us as a guide. When not being hospitable to visitors, he involved himself in efforts to prevent antique smuggling. Occasionally, however, he would organise some musical performances and arts and calligraphy exhibitions in an attempt to remind Yuantan residents of the intended mission of the centre. For him the reason

---

THE CULTURAL CENTRE

The middle-aged director was not having an easy time.

My ancestral home is nearby Wanghe village where livelihood was based on rice, fish and bamboo. I'm the third of five children in a peasant family. I was the one chosen to have proper schooling and I got as far as junior middle school. I didn't take the exams for senior middle school because I thought my family wouldn't be able to afford sending me there. I became a primary school teacher. Soon I was back at school myself - the state paid for me to go part time to a vocational agricultural school. This is when I got my interests in music, basketball and painting. Then the Cultural Revolution broke out and everything was chaotic. I went off to Beijing and was amongst the eighth group of red guards to be greeted by Chairman Mao. My experience and courage both grew. At that time there was fighting everywhere, but I didn't join in. In 1968 many young city folk came to the village in response to Chairman Mao's great call. I reckon that the idea of getting re-education from the poor and lower-middle peasants - i.e. sending the youth out of the cities - was just a ruse to solve unemployment. These kids added a heavy burden in the village. Of all my classmates who studied agricultural machinery, only one in 20 actually put their knowledge to use. In 1970, I went off to Anqing Teachers College for a year, and then became a physics teacher. But I hankered after some kind of cultural work and ended up in Yuantan Cultural Centre.

continued...

---

for the decline of the cultural centre was simply the low priority accorded institutions which did not generate revenue. The authorities regarded the money allocated to the centre as unproductive costs, so a reduction in its budget represented a welcome saving. The director informed us that the decline in healthy cultural work had resulted in a revival of old superstitions and in the renewed popularity of mah-jong, gambling and similar - to his mind - decadent pursuits. Formerly, apparently, the cultural centre provided a form of adult education, especially for the peasantry. In fact, Yuantan did have rich cultural resources including handicrafts and folk drama although these were disappearing we were told with the death of the older generation.

The traditional marriages, which revived after the Cultural Revolution, still occurred in Yuantan, although rather less frequently it

I got married at 30 - late for the countryside. I found a girl from a hill village who had some education. She was a grain farmer. We have two children. They'll carry on and do the things I was never able to do. In the Cultural Centre my pay was really little at first - 22 yuan a month in 1974 and just over 40 yuan in the early 1980s. It's now just 280 yuan monthly - still low. But I like the work in the Cultural Centre: it is really important for the general public.

Between 1974 and 1976, cultural life seemed very rich. Every level of administration had a performance group. Then there were few TVs. People were organised to make their own entertainment - singing and dancing. After 1976 things cooled, but Anqing's Cultural Bureau gave us 13,000 yuan to build a new centre. It was a fine building - the best in the town. But 14 years on, now its the most decrepit in the town. Cultural work hasn't been taken seriously - only the economy is thought to be important.

seemed than in the early years of the reform period. According to the accounts we heard from the older generation, such a marriage in Yuantan was a complex business, and often required the services of a matchmaker. Once the go-between effected an introduction between boy and girl, the fiancee's parents and relatives paid a visit to the boy's family. The purpose of this reconnaissance was economic. The parents attempted to determine the conditions into which their daughter would be delivered. They wanted to see a big house, plenty of land, and a well situated establishment near a road. If conditions were considered satisfactory the visiting family would stay for lunch. Otherwise they would return home and call the engagement off. Once the agreement of the girl's family was secured, her uncles would be invited to make an inspection visit of their own. If all was approved, betrothal began officially, with an exchange of gifts. This inaugurated a period of courtship which could last from a few months to several years, although pregnancy occasionally expedited matters. If the couple realised they were not suited during the courtship period they could terminate their relationship. This usually led to a good deal of increasingly bad-tempered haggling as the respective families met in an attempt to thrash out what each had given the other and how everyone should be compensated.

However, traditions were changing, and 'love marriages' were on the increase. This at least made it relatively simple to end a relationship. Nonetheless, marriage was still regarded as a serious business and preparations were thorough and detailed, particularly in the countryside.

The future groom's family chose the wedding date only after consulting his horoscope. Once the date was set, the village elder wrote invitations which were conveyed by the go-between to each of the relatives. If the couple had met each other by themselves, then one representative was selected from each family on the groom's side to attend the wedding. The groom's family were responsible for preparing presents for the wedding guests, traditionally small items like pork, cigarettes and spirits, and also for raising a cash gift for the couple of around 5,000 yuan. For their part, the bride's relations provided furniture and consumer goods for the couple. On the day of the wedding a banquet took place, after which the bride entered and became subsumed in the life of her new husband's family. In rare cases this process was reversed. In these *dao cha men* marriages, the husband moved into the wife's house, the wife's family covered all the wedding costs, and the children took her family name. Such an arrangement was unusual, however, and occurred only in response to a particular set of circumstances. Usually, it was because the new husband was relatively poor and the wife was an only child, and thus had to remain with her parents to look after their land, a responsibility which she could henceforth share with her husband. The rise in the number of young people who preferred to sort out their own matrimonial affairs, however, was yet another sign of change in Yuantan. But the occurrence of *dao cha men* marriages also showed that the old traditions had the flexibility needed for survival. Significantly, even though people had the freedom to follow their own matrimonial path, many still chose the traditional way.

The cost of a funeral had increased in recent years. Funeral ceremonies were becoming ever more extravagant. A 44 year-old primary school teacher told us:

A funeral can now cost over 2,000 yuan. The local custom is to wrap the corpse in a piece of cloth and place it on some high ground. After the flesh has rotted away, the bones are collected, put into a coffin and buried in a plot bought at between 100 and 200 yuan. Poor families usually just bury their relatives on any vacant land they can find in the hills. But the increase in burial sites means a reduction in land, so the authorities have been advocating cremation. Many farmers do not accept this practice and have occasionally removed bodies by force from the crematorium. Personally, I think cremation is better. Too many grave sites reduce our land resources.

In Yuantan we observed a steady stream of people going to the local temples. In the Diaoyu temple on the bank of the Dasha river many of the visitors burned incense and prayed for good fortune before a statue of the Buddha. Traditional thanksgiving involved firecrackers, and the offer of a chicken, whose Chinese name *ji* is a homonym for the character for luck. Some visitors to the temple asked for an oracle by drawing bamboo slips. There was a well known Taoist temple called '*Sanzu Si*' in Qianshan, the county town. To reach it visitors had to climb a long, steeply ascending mountain path, but still the site was often very busy. Many local people apparently believed in the effectiveness of the bamboo sticks found there.

Future Developments

For the 'Planning Report for the Urban System in Qianshan', the county was divided into three economic regions. Yuantan town, in the county's northern region, had been identified as one of the two key towns for development. It was recommended that Yuantan should stabilise its grain production and diversify its economic base. It suggested a further diversification of agricultural crops, an expansion of forestry, the development of quarrying, the manufacture of construction materials and the general development of industry and commerce to take advantage of local transport links. According to the official Ten Year Plan for Yuantan, by 2002 the economy was projected to grow sufficiently to increase per capita income to 1,200 yuan. It was envisaged that the town core would develop into the regional administrative and economic centre, with particular emphasis on commerce and high technology industries. We were told that many of the planned projects needed huge sums of money for investment and that higher priority was to be accorded the key township enterprises. The objective here was to add value during the production process, which required more sophisticated technology. This it was felt was the surest way to increase tax revenues for the town and general prosperity for Yuantan. A good example was the magnetic materials factory. This could only manufacture semi-finished products selling at 2,000-3,000 yuan per tonne, while finished goods would have sold for 16,000-18,000 yuan per tonne. Therefore the town government was considering a further investment of six million yuan, and negotiations with the Construction Bank for a loan were already in progress. Another example was the plastics factory, again to enable it to manufacture finished goods of higher added value than was presently the case. For this project the Agricultural Bank has already agreed to provide five million yuan.

While the town's major industries were clearly to be the main recipients of investment, we were told by the town authorities that they were also to provide appropriate financial help to village-run and other small enterprises. It was planned to allocate some 800,000 yuan for such enterprises. Particular attention was to be paid to three villages which had no enterprises at all. Between 80,000 and 100,000 yuan was to be made available for each of these villages to set up some small township enterprises. One activity which the town and county authorities wished to promote in the region was tourism, exploiting both the scenic resources of the mountainous area and the excellent communications network. Local leaders were fond of referring to Yuantan as the 'gateway to the Wanxi Dabieshan range'. Certainly, our time in the near-by hills and mountains persuaded us that the region had great potential for tourism. Tourism from within China had already developed to a limited extent, but the accessibility of the area by water and air provided opportunities for attracting international visitors. An improvement in the standard and quantity of accommodation in Yuantan could perhaps be the first stage in the development of a valuable tourist industry in the *zhen*.

4　Shengze

Location and History

Shengze *zhen* is located in the economically well developed region of south Jiangsu province, some 90 kilometres south-west of Shanghai. Shengze is the biggest town under the jurisdiction of Wujiang city which is situated about 30 kilometres to the north-west. Wujiang itself comes under the prefectural level municipality of Suzhou. Shengze *zhen* occupies about 70 square kilometres and embraces eight surrounding villages. The urban core area occupied around 20 square kilometres in the mid-1990s but was expanding rapidly.

The history of the town was summarised for us by a resident with a long-standing interest in local affairs who had edited the official history. He had entered Nanjing Normal College to study Chinese, but after a year was sent to the countryside to work, later returning to study at Shanghai Normal University. Most of his teaching career was spent at Wujiang's Silk College. Shengze remained a small village throughout the Tang (618-907), Song (960-1279) and early Ming (1368-1644) dynasties. During these periods other towns in the region were experiencing surges of prosperity. The reasons for Shengze's lack of development were probably its isolation from south Jiangsu's major urban centres and the distance to the north-south conduit of the Grand Canal. A propensity to flooding and large areas of marshland also made Shengze an unattractive proposition for agriculture. It seems that Shengze first began to attract notice during the middle period of the Ming dynasty, about 500 years ago, which makes it a comparative latecomer in Jiangsu. Change came with government encouragement of silkworm husbandry, to which the local land was well suited. Henceforth, Shengze's history became inextricably linked with the silk industry and the town is known in China as one of the four traditional 'silk capitals' along with Suzhou, Hangzhou and Huzhou. Shengze's isolation, which previously had been an obstacle to development, became an advantage during the frequent intervals of strife and civil commotion. From the Jiajing era of the Ming (1522-1566), Shengze rose on the proceeds of household handicraft silk making. The men cultivated the mulberry trees; the women wove the silk. By the end of the Ming dynasty, Shengze was reputed to be a thriving place with a large number of traders, some big workshops and a workforce of highly trained silk workers. By the Qianlong era of the Qing, it had become the largest market town in Wujiang county. During the conflict-ridden Xianfen era, a class of business refugees from Jiangsu and Zhejiang provinces congregated in Shengze giving its market an even greater regional importance. Further economic development occurred in Shengze during the Taiping rebellion (1850-1864). At this time the economy in the south of Jiangsu had collapsed because insurgent Taiping forces had destroyed other towns such as Suzhou and Wujiang. Shengze, however, appeased the Taiping and pledged loyalty to them, thereby avoiding the ravages that befell neighbouring towns. Shengze not only escaped destruction, but also received investment and skilled workers from towns embroiled in the warfare. A combination of relative political stability and a skilled workforce meant that Shengze's silk industry was well placed to develop further. After the Taiping was crushed, in the mid-1860s, Qing troops rampaged through south Jiangsu under Li Hongzhang, destroying those towns which had been loyal to the Taiping. Shengze was allegedly saved by the intervention of a British customs official from Shanghai, called Yiluqi locally. His assessment that Shengze was China's major silk production centre prevented its destruction by the imperial troops. Although the fortunes of the silk industry have fluctuated since the 1860s - and still do so in the modern era - Shengze's status as China's silk capital remained intact until the 1920s. Thereafter, Shengze suffered from a lack of electricity, and it lost its competitive position: resurgency has been a feature of the post-Mao reform period.

In 1949 the population of Shengze's was 23,000, but declined in the succeeding 30 years with the conscription of many local people to work in the interior and the later rustication of young people and cadres. Also, we were told that a larger proportion of the population than elsewhere had starved during the three famine years, 1959-1961. From the 1970s onwards, however, Shengze had undergone profound changes, initially associated with the revival of the silk industry. Although silk remains the town's principal industry there is now a diverse range of industrial and commercial activities. As well as being the largest town in Wujiang, Shengze is regarded as the economic pillar of the district.

Physical Environment

Shengze lies within the Delta Sub-region of the Middle and Lower Yangzi Plain Natural Region (Zhao Songqiao, 1986). The whole of the delta area was submerged during the early Holocene. Subsequently, sea level dropped and the area has received massive accumulations of material from the Yangzi and other rivers, and also from offshore. The whole area is very low lying (mostly < 10 metres above sea level) and is criss-crossed by numerous natural and artificial waterways. The density of the river network is about 6.5 kilometres per square kilometre (Zhao Songqiao, 1986). This area has one of the longest histories of continuous crop cultivation in China, particularly of paddy rice. Although large-scale urban encroachment on agricultural land has been an important feature of the post-1980 period, the delta area remains a very important one for crop production. Soils in this alluvial-lacustrine area are mainly eutric gleysols. They are characterized by a high water table for much of the year. The shores of the large and shallow Taihu Lake are about 20 kilometres to the north-west and there are numerous small lakes much closer to the town core. Nine rivers and streams once ran through the town, although urban construction has covered two of them. Channels link the nearby lakes with the Beijing to Hangzhou canal, which is three kilometres to the east.

Climatically, the area falls within the humid subtropical zone. There are four distinct seasons. Winters are cool and summers are hot. Shanghai, which is just 65 kilometres to the north-east, provides a useful reference for conditions in Shengze. In winter the temperature is usually above freezing point and the mean January temperature is around 3°C. July, with an average temperature of 29°C is the hottest month. Frost occurs on average about 40 days per year. Rainfall is plentiful (over 1100 mm annually). Appreciable amounts of rain fall in every month but there are three distinct rainy seasons (called locally, spring rain, plum rain and autumn rain). On average, rain falls on 131 days every year, but over 70 per cent of the total falls in the period April to September. A long growing season, abundant sunshine and rainfall, and deep alluvial soils combine to make the Yangzi delta area one of the most productive in China.

The southern part of China's eastern seaboard and adjacent inland areas is subject to periodic typhoon activity. (Typhoon is the term applied to intense tropical cyclones originating in the north-western Pacific: to be designated as a typhoon in China windspeed must exceed 17.2 metres per second - Beaufort Scale 8 - in the centre of the cyclone.) Most typhoons occur between June and November, but are concentrated in the July-

September period. In times of prolonged heavy rainfall and high surface water levels, the local area, including the town core area, is liable to flood.

Shengze's Appearance

Shengze's town core initially occupied a one kilometre stretch along side the Shi river. In the 1950s the streets were gradually widened, and in the 1970s the river was filled to became Shengze Avenue. Crossing the avenue at its mid-point is Shengxin Road, the town's other major thoroughfare. The two main roads cross at Dongfang Square, which forms the central point of the town. At the end of 1988, a thirteen-storey building, Dongfang Plaza, was constructed on the square. Before it stands a statue of a female silk worker, a siren for the town's economic base. To the south of Shengze Avenue are some of the old residential districts. The silk mills, and their newly constructed worker accommodation, lie to the north. Shengze Avenue runs between the town's two lakes, Dongbaiyang and Xibaiyang, and serves as the town's main retail corridor. The biggest market of the town is at the west end of Shengze Avenue. The town's major public facilities, including the schools, hospital, hotels and bus station are concentrated along Shengxin Road. The intersection of Shengxin Road and Shengze Avenue divides the town into four parts, with the Oriental Silk Market being located in the southwest quadrant. To the east another major highway, Dongfang Boulevard, runs parallel to Shengxin Road. The area of the town core has been steadily growing in recent years and is projected to be 20 square kilometres in 2000. More and more of the town's old urban heart was set to be destroyed to make way for factories, shopping centres and new residential neighbourhoods.

From the early days of the People's Republic until the late 1970s the slogan 'production first, livelihood second' dominated government policy, and precious little new construction was devoted to improving the quality of life. This philosophy began to change in the 1980s. A master plan for Shengze's town core was produced in 1983 and was gradually implemented. By the mid-1990s, centred on the Oriental Silk Market, was a 12 hectare area known as the Shengze Silk Business City. This was divided into six districts and 800 lots. The whole south-west quadrant of the town was being developed into a trade centre, while the northern and eastern parts of the town, located at some distance from the residential areas, were zoned for manufacturing industry.

In the past, each of the major silk mills had its own housing for workers nearby. The existing Xinhua, Xinming and Xinchun neighbourhoods were named after well-known silk producing enterprises in the town. In the late 1980s, the local authorities built another four small neighbourhoods to cater for silk workers. The Town East Neighbourhood, Taoyuan New Village, Qiaobei New Village and Luyang New Village each occupied an area of around 12 hectares. Two 'villa areas' of middle and upper income housing, Yingxiang and Bisheng, were being built during our visit. The old town was also being redeveloped. Old houses were being demolished, roads widened and tower blocks constructed. The short-term plan was to remove practically all vestiges of the old town.

The town leadership had also embarked on a wide range of infrastructure projects, which were in various stages of development when we visited. Notable environmental developments included a new waste-water treatment plant and water treatment works, and the completion of a new ring road to reduce urban congestion (we were told that the road would cost 50 million yuan). A combined heat and power electrical generating station, paid for by a business levy imposed by Wujiang city government, was nearing completion, and was expected to be more efficient, and less polluting than existing power generating facilities based on individual coal-fired boilers. In addition, over 200,000 yuan had been invested in various 'greening' projects. By the early 21st century, therefore, Shengze's metamorphosis into a completely modern small town should be virtually complete. The only vestiges of the town which existed here just 15 years previously will be a few old, hopefully renovated, residential properties in the old town area.

Local Administration

The head of the town, whose career had previously embraced coal mining, accountancy and collecting statistics prior to town management, outlined the structure of Shengze's town management. As elsewhere, he was in charge of all the town's activities, but in practice he divided the responsibilities between a number of deputies whom he met formally once a month when they reported back on their work. Collectively, their activities embraced law and order, technology, labour, birth control, environmental protection, town construction, land management, and sanitation. The state had provided an employment quota of 81 persons for the town's government, but apparently the number employed was around one hundred.

Elections were held once every three years to the town's Party committee and to its administration, both are which are under the leadership of the Party committee and government of Wujiang city. Both Shengze town and Wujiang city conformed to the so-called 'Suzhou Model', under which the Party committee had specific oversight of all the town's administrative and commercial activities. Apart from some cosmetic adjustments, this arrangement had remained unchanged during the reform era. The town's Party committee consisted of a Party secretary, nine deputies, and some ordinary committee members. The nine deputies were also either township (*xiang*) heads or deputy heads, and had other key administrative functions in addition.

Economic affairs were the responsibility of the town government's all important Agriculture, Industry and Commerce Company. This group had a board of directors and a management committee but operated under the direct leadership of the Party committee. Shengze's Party secretary held the post of executive director while the deputies alternated as directors. The Party secretary was also the company's general manager. Within this holding company structure were smaller operations charged with governance of the town's various economic activities, including agriculture, trade, industry and services.

Shengze's people's congress was set up in 1954. The chairman of its standing committee ran the day-to-day business of the congress and was also a member of the Wujiang people's congress. Township heads and deputies were also elected by the congress. We were told that the average age of the leading officials of Shengze was 44 years. They all combined grass-roots work experience with high school or college education, often studying for qualifications while working. We found them all to be youthful and energetic in outlook. Apart from the enterprises owned by Wujiang municipal government, such as the Oriental Silk Market, all business and social affairs were the responsibility of the town authority and its subordinate organisations. All the government departments in the town had their corresponding superiors in Wujiang city and Jiangsu provincial government. Issues within the jurisdiction of the town authority were dealt with locally. Otherwise they were moved on up the hierarchy.

Demographic Aspects

Matters concerning births, deaths and migration were dealt with by residential committees within the town core, and by notaries in the countryside. Both reported to their local police station. By the mid-1990s the registered population was around 74,000, of which 32,000 were urban residents. However, there was some doubt about the actual population. If unregistered and temporarily permitted migrants were included, the officially estimated total population in the mid-1990s was over 110,000. However, the Party representative at Shengze police station told us he believed even this underestimated the true figure by some 30,000.

The birth rate in Shengze peaked in 1988 at approximately 17 births per thousand. Despite some decline, the birth rate in the rural hinterland was still higher than in the town core area, which showed that traditional rural attitudes towards fertility remained. Since 1963 the death rate had declined slightly, from about nine to just under seven per thousand. The highest death rate since 1949, about 20 per thousand, was recorded in 1961, the last of the three major famine years.

Migration has long been a key element in Shengze's demographic profile. In prosperous times during the Qing dynasty, for example, large numbers of immigrants were attracted to the town from as far away as Shandong and Shanxi. More recently, in the 1960s, emigration from Shengze was much greater than immigration because of the large-scale rustication of educated residents and the relocation of people to work in the interior provinces. The number of immigrants began to increase again after 1973, and by 1978 had surpassed replacement levels. Out-migration remained greater than in-migration in the surrounding rural areas, however, as the urban core continued to attract workers. The flow of labour to the town core was greatly encouraged in the 1980s after registration policies were relaxed in an attempt to address the problem of labour shortages in the rapidly developing silk industry. Initially, labour for the silk mills was provided mostly by local peasant farmers, but in the late 1980s it became clear that this source was insufficient to meet the growing demands of the industry. Accordingly, labour was recruited from the northern part of Jiangsu, as well as other provinces.

In theory, the household registration system in Shengze had remained in place since the establishment of the People's Republic. From 1964 until the 1980s only a small proportion of the local rural population was allowed to acquire urban household registration, but since 1984 peasant farmers were allowed to reside in cities and towns, provided they did not rely on public food subsidies. When food coupons were abolished in the second half of 1992, the perception of the importance of household registration changed, because it now related only to enrollment in schools and to employment.

It was clear that there were different categories of unregistered workers in Shengze. At one extreme there were people who had lived in the town for some years. It was such people who provided the silk industry with the major part of its work force. At the other extreme were migrant workers - the floating population - who moved around in search of work, typically in construction or seasonal farm work. Locally registered residents expressed mixed feelings about the large population of unregistered immigrants, and did not always differentiate between the various categories. Most officials we spoke to claimed that the shortage of labour constrained the pace of development in the town, and that more workers were still required. On the other hand, there was a general view that migrant labourers were responsible for the increase in crime that had occurred in recent years.

After 1993, Shengze operated a specialised immigration management office which issued transient resident permits to outsiders visiting the town for more than a week. A high proportion of permits were issued to contract labourers from Henan, Anhui and Sichuan provinces. There was also a substantial number of commercial travellers and traders from Wuhan (Hubei), Wenzhou (Zhejiang) and Shijiazhuang (Hebei). Within the town there was a service station to which immigrant workers were supposed to report on arrival. Such workers were officially required to hold an identification card and a letter of introduction, both issued by the government in their home town, before they could take up employment in Shengze. Once employed, they registered with the appropriate administrative office. Private enterprises in Shengze remained largely outside the official scheme: they normally recruited their own workers and administered the official registration.

While labour shortage was widely acknowledged to be a problem for Shengze, the swelling number of residents put a large strain on the town and its infrastructure. We were informed that on any day about half of Shengze's population would be in the town core. For Shengze's governor, the only way to avoid the inevitable problems created by an increasing number of residents, and simultaneously address the labour shortage problem, was to increase investment in technology. We saw evidence of this approach in some of the enterprises we visited. Typically, the enterprise would be a cooperative venture involving a company based outside the town which required more space to develop new factories. Shengze, with its proximity to Shanghai was very well placed to attract investment. However, the shift towards more technological, and less labour intensive industrial operations raised important social questions.

Another distinctive feature of Shengze's demographic profile was the high proportion of female residents. According to the census data, even in 1982 Shengze had over 132 women for every 100 men in the 18-30 age range, while in the 1990s young women comprised about 70 per cent of the immigrant population. This gender imbalance was due to the preference of the silk industry for young female workers. The key role that women played historically in the silk industry probably explained why the preference for male off-spring was very much less apparent in Shengze than is usual elsewhere in China. In fact, effective local birth reduction programmes were initiated in the 1950s, long before the one-child policy of the 1980s. Between 1971 and 1986, the average annual birth rate in the town was 11 per thousand. Births rose initially after 1979 due to the large number of people returning from the countryside to settle down and raise families. Yet despite this, and a lowering of the age limits for marriage in 1984, Shengze managed to stay within its quota.

Population control in Shengze was the operational responsibility of the local police. The force was split into rural and urban divisions, each of which was responsible for monitoring the population in their area of jurisdiction. Four police officers in the rural part of the *zhen* and three police officers in the town-core area were employed full time on population registration. Our chief informant on birth control issues was a Party secretary from one of the district offices. Birth control work amongst town residents was apparently fairly easy, because people were familiar with the policy after years of propaganda, and probably because of the preference shown for females in many roles within the silk industry. There was no big problem in the surrounding countryside either, although farmers were often less willing to conform than town core residents. However, the policy was becoming more flexible as couples who were single children themselves were now allowed to have a second child. Economic growth and in-migration had brought with them the new problem of managing birth control amongst migrants, who often claimed they had been granted permission by their home town to have an extra child. The large proportion of young women among the immigrant population made the problem particularly acute. A new development associated with increasing affluence was the adoption of children, who were usually born to migrant women and then abandoned. It was usual for

---

LOCAL GOVERNMENT

This middle-aged female respondent was employed in one of the neighbourhood (*jiedao*) offices of Shengze. From the beginning to now she has been guided along her career path by the local government.

My family has been in Shengze for generations. Before Liberation my father was in the silk business and afterwards he was given a job in a state grain shop. My mother went into a weaving mill and she now lives with me. I graduated from Shengze Middle School in 1963 and then got a job in a street-run enterprise. But in 1970 this was closed because of the 'sending down' movement. Later the same unit was reopened as a township industry and I was made accountant. Then the town decided to set up Chaoyang Clothing and I was appointed manager. I did this for eight years until my health wouldn't stand it. The factory was based on almost no investment - just 900 yuan initially. The workers were mainly housewives and they brought their own sewing machines with them. After leaving in 1982 I went to work for the industrial bureau. There my health was restored and I was moved to a packaging factory. This was another enterprise set up by housewives and its products were poor quality so the burden on me was heavy. I became ill again in 1992 and had to rest for a couple of years. Because of my poor health the town moved me to this Street office.

I'm the deputy Party secretary of the Street office; under it are 26 residents' committees. I'm in charge of propaganda, organisation, personnel and women's affairs. The latter is of course mainly family planning. In this, the most difficult part is controlling the situation amongst incomers from other regions. We require these people to apply for a birth quota from their place of origin. Otherwise our own quota will be exceeded. Adoption has become one of the main issues. If local people have a son, they would want to adopt a daughter. If they have a daughter, they would seek to adopt a son.

continued...

---

adopting couples who already had one child to select a second child of the opposite gender.

Household structure in Shengze reflected a fairly rigidly imposed one-child policy in the area and a trend towards nuclear, rather than extended families. Sixty per cent of the households in our survey contained

Family conditions are now better here and people have got the money. The adoptees are usually abandoned babies born to migrant labourers. Family planning for the local residents is easier because the government's policies have not been applied for many years and people have got used to them. And there are no big problems with the people in Shengze's rural areas. Under certain circumstances we allow a couple to have a second child. For instance, if both are their parents' only child, they can try for a second child of their own.

Frankly, the migrants are from poor places and they're of low quality all round. When I was in the factory we recruited some. They were incompetent and lazy. At that time there weren't many migrants here. When development got under way later on, large numbers of construction workers came in. Public security went downhill. To help the regular police and guards, we set up our own vigilante group to protect property, and have invited several dozen retirees to join our patrols. Though they aren't physically strong they manage to pose some kind of a threat.

three or less occupants, 40 per cent of households contained four or five occupants, while 10 per cent had six or more occupants.

Work and Income

For the area known as Shengze *zhen* the number of people employed in agriculture had progressively declined since 1982 as the opportunities for off-farm employment had risen. Reflecting the comparatively recent change in Shengze's economy, only one respondent in our survey of 130 residents was categorised as a peasant. About 30 per cent of respondents were primarily industrial workers and over 30 per cent were either professionals or cadres. Interestingly, over 25 per cent of Shengze respondents were assigned to the 'other' occupational group because they appeared to be involved in many, or else undisclosed remunerative activities. Local residents who were employed in textiles or textile machinery plants tended to work in managerial or supervisory roles, for example, in accountancy, quality inspection, sales and marketing. Surprisingly, most of the front line workers in industry were immigrants. Private ownership of businesses in Shengze remained largely confined to the retail sector and restaurant trade. The numbers changed frequently and it was difficult to obtain reliable data. However, the record shows that in 1982, there were over 40 individual businesses. By 1987 this number had risen to over 1,200 and by the end of our survey was probably in excess of 7,000. The growth in this sector, we were told, had been promoted by the new Oriental Silk Market and the town-run Oriental Silk City.

Although Shengze remained a rural town, the development of the silk industry and other commercial activities meant that young people in the town's country districts had come to regard working on the land as almost inconceivable. The likelihood was also that both parents were employed in the silk industry. The expectation for many of Shengze's young therefore was that they would take well paid posts in management, marketing or quality assurance. The saying '*wu gong bu fu*' (no factory job, no wealth) was once a statement of aspiration. Now, most people took a good standard of living for granted. Those who expected rather more went into business, setting up stalls in the Oriental Silk Market or Shengze's Silk City, trading in silk, chemical fibres or other textile products. The talk here was all about who had just struck a great deal, who had a fortune stashed away and who had just built a villa. Silk trading had brought great wealth to a number of people, and their success had influenced the wider culture of the town. Perhaps the saying now should be 'no business, no wealth'.

In our survey, a third of respondents received an income of 4,000-7,000 yuan annually (a third received less than 4,000 and a third received more than 7000 yuan). The annual salary income for the ordinary government clerks was around 10,000 yuan while the figure reported to us for migrant workers was between 4,000 and 5,000 yuan. We met factory workers doing semi-skilled work who earned over 7,000 yuan a year. Disparities in wealth were conspicuous in Shengze. Six of the business families we met earned over 50,000 yuan per year, and three of these claimed an income of over 100,000 yuan annually. Informally we heard that some private businesses earned more than a million yuan annually. Others with a high income were those contracted to manage factories. At the other end of the scale, however, three of our households reportedly brought in nothing at all. In our survey we found that wages in Shengze's rural area were only about 75 per cent of those in the town core. In general, salaries in the town-run enterprises exceeded those in the public and county collective enterprises, although the former did not provide pension and welfare benefits. The wages paid to employees provided a fairly reliable indicator of enterprise profitability. We heard that certain public and county collective enterprises, e.g. the Silk Printing and Dyeing

Factory, Satin Printing No. 1 and No. 2 Factories and Xinming Silk Factory had all been very productive and had been able to reward their workers with pay rises in the recent past whereas salaries in silk machinery and equipment factories had remained comparatively low. In response to our question concerning income satisfaction, more than 40 per cent of respondents claimed they were satisfied with their current income, fewer than a quarter claimed they were dissatisfied, while a third thought the present income level was 'so-so' (*mama huhu*).

The impression gained was that work and enterprise were well rewarded in Shengze and that a strong work ethic existed among those we interviewed. Over half our respondents believed improvements in their life would come from their own efforts. The remainder attributed economic advancement to luck or other circumstances. The relatively high purchasing power of Shengze residents was clearly evident in the range, quality, and price of goods in the stores, as well as in the more conspicuous emblems of high income, notably the new spacious villas on the edge of the town. Patterns of consumption were similar to those in the big cities. Affluence had not appeared to have dimmed ambition. One clothes retailer told us that an annual income of 100,000 yuan was only middle class by local standards and that 'business was the business of Shengze: all people of talent and ability turned to it naturally as a source of wealth and a means of self expression'. We were told that the Shengze Town Annals recorded that Shengze people were traditionally 'not interested in higher degrees, but keen on higher earnings'. One of our key informants on environmental issues stated that the younger of his two daughters had decided to go into business like her sister, despite having a teaching degree, because she would earn two to three times as much money. A young clerk from the local government told us that he would like to run a shop similar to the one of his former school mates, again because he would earn much more than his current salary.

Agriculture

A combination of warmth, moisture, and fertile soils mean that the region is well endowed for crop cultivation. The main natural obstacle to cultivation is a vulnerability to waterlogging which makes drainage a necessity. Paradoxically, occasional droughts occur. We were told that an extended period of dry weather in 1994 would have resulted in a poor harvest without efficient water management. In general, the region's population had been able to feed itself with relative ease in most years.

Shengze, with a comparatively small population drawing sustenance from a large area of rich agricultural land, has long been known as a town of 'fish and rice'. After 1950, however, a series of administrative boundary changes separated Shengze's urban core from its agricultural hinterland, leaving it dependent on small plots given over to vegetable production. As industry developed in Shengze this land was reduced still further. At the end of 1989, further administrative changes restored an agricultural hinterland to the town, a change that permitted the planning and implementation of large scale commercial agriculture in the *zhen*. By 1994, over 42,000 mu of land was under cultivation. However, with a population, including migrants, of well over 100,000 the per capita amount of cultivable land in the *zhen* stood at around 0.4 mu in the mid-1990s and would inevitably decrease. However, the town leaders repeatedly reassured us that they took agriculture very seriously and that the *zhen* could supply its own needs.

The main food crops were rice, wheat, oil-seed rape and vegetables. In addition, Shengze's cultivated area still had room for mulberry trees, on which the town's industrial and commercial development was historically based. An aquatic area of some 10,500 mu was used for aquaculture, particularly for perch and whitebait, which apparently enjoyed a wide reputation within China. Approximately 25,000 pigs and a million chickens and ducks were produced annually in Shengze.

The growth of local industry and the tantalising prospect of higher wages for easier work caused a migration of young and enthusiastic farmers to the towns, leaving many household plots neglected and even abandoned. Those who remained on the land tended to be 'the old, the women and the very young'. For the sake of food security the township enterprises acted to reverse this decline. In the early 1990s some three million yuan was spent on improvements designed to make farming more productive and better rewarded. The town leadership also centralised the supply of agricultural necessities and encouraged farmers to reduce the number of yearly harvests to one. Money was also been invested in improving the water supply and in coordinating plant protection. As a result of these measures, the needs of the local and transient population - approximately 10 million jin of grain annually - could be met. In fact annual output from the *zhen* was normally well above national procurement quotas. Agriculture was moving towards intensive and large-scale production. There had been a consolidation of enterprises, with a few large producers controlling many of what were nominally household plots. We were told that in 1994, one big farm in Yangshan village had planted over 170 mu, had met its quotas, and made 70,000 yuan in income. Such large-scale farming could provide higher incomes than employment in the TVEs, although the work was usually more arduous. However, farm income levels of this magnitude were only possible because the costs of farm machinery, crop protection and irrigation were all taken care of by village enterprises and many of the tasks were undertaken by a cooperative network established by the village leadership. In fact, TVEs had moved from subsidising farmers for the sake of food security to funding the development of more business-like agricultural enterprises for the benefit of the local economy as a whole.

The income of farmers was secured by a contract with their local village leadership, which undertook to subvent them in the event of natural disasters. This insurance removed the uncertainty from farming, a vital incentive to retain the remaining large scale producers on the land. Another recent feature of agriculture in Shengze, as elsewhere in the more economically advanced areas of China, was the use of teams of migrant labourers to carry out the farm work under contract to the town. As remarked earlier, very few of Shengze's inhabitants worked on the land by choice.

Although most villagers now worked off-farm, it was quite common for them to keep some land for personal food production. However, in Shengze *zhen* as a whole only 20 per cent of respondents in our survey provided their own grain. In the main, the contracted land of the household responsibility system had come under the management of the larger farms, which employed seasonal labour at harvest and other busy times, or else entirely contracted out the work. However, the village cooperative network maintained an overview of developments in the area under their jurisdiction. Animal husbandry, fish farming and vegetable production were also collectively organised. While local supplies of meat and fish were more than adequate, vegetable production was not yet sufficient to meet the needs of Shengze's ever-swelling population.

Industry and Commerce

At the onset of reform in the late 1970s the value of agricultural output exceeded that of the non-agricultural sector. It is a measure of the rate of industrial development in Shengze that while agriculture remained important to the town in absolute terms, its relative contribution to the town's economy had progressively declined. We were told that in the mid-1990s this value was just one-thirtieth of total output value. Until the

1930s, silk production in Shengze relied entirely on manually powered silk looms. However, Shengze's connection to a supply of electricity following the completion of the Suzhou Electricity and Gas Station in 1935 instigated the gradual transformation of a largely home based, craft like activity to a factory based industrial process. Industrial scale silk production developed slowly as the industry was suffering from the protectionist trade policies in place in Europe and the United States in the 1930s, and then the upheavals associated with the civil war, anti-Japanese war and Second World War. In consequence, many of the new powered looms were modified for cotton production. It was not until 1958 that all cotton production ceased in the town under an official directive.

In the early years of the People's Republic, silk was still produced on handlooms at the household level and was coordinated by the state organisation, the China Silk Company. After collectivisation, some households managed to maintain production as a sideline, but in 1958 they were amalgamated to form the Shengze Commune Silk Textiles Mill. Although this pioneering enterprise failed two years later, brigade-run mills quickly emerged throughout the district. It was these enterprises which provided the basis for the much more entrepreneurial silk industry which rapidly developed during the reform period. By 1987 there were nearly 50 silk fabric enterprises, 10 of which belonged to the town while most of the rest were run by the local villages. During the 1950s exports slowly resumed, being managed by a variety of state trading houses over the years. By 1979, export earnings exceeded domestic sales for the first time and several of the county owned factories were dedicated entirely to exporting. The managing director of the Shengze General Company for Agriculture, Industry and Commerce told us that in the mid-1990s the town accounted for one-sixth of the natural silk and about one-tenth of the artificial silk exported from China each year. In general, real silk products are earmarked for exports while the artificial product is sold domestically. During the period of our visits, silk production and ancillary enterprises accounted for approximately 80 per cent of the value of the town's industrial output and the silk industry was the chief employer in the town.

An important feature of the silk industry's development in the 1980s and 1990s had been the steadily increasing production of artificial silk. In fact synthetic silk accounted for most of Shengze's output and 80 per cent of business in the Oriental Silk Market during the period of our visit. The trend towards artificial silk was due to the state's monopoly of silk production, from 'egg to market'. The state prescribed the number of silkworm cocoons to be bought each year and imposed strict limits on the amount of silk exported. State production contracts for natural silk went predominantly to large, publicly owned mills, which forced township enterprises to specialise in the synthetic alternative. Nonetheless, the quality of the local synthetic product was high enough for such discriminating export markets as Japan.

While the silk industry enjoyed a period of unprecedented prosperity during the 1980s and early 1990s, during our visits in the mid-1990s we were aware that it was not operating at full capacity, and that the town was experiencing a sharp drop in demand for its products. A symptom of this downturn in the silk economy was that the town's principal luxury hotel, built to accommodate (and impress) buyers from elsewhere, was almost completely empty.

The silk industry in Shengze encompassed printing and dyeing, as well as weaving. A wide range of finished products was also manufactured there. A feature of the local industry was the great diversity in the size of factories, the standard of equipment, and conditions and rewards to workers. On the one hand we visited large, newly built enterprises which contained the most up-to-date equipment - typically imported from Germany, Japan or Italy - with relatively few employees working under comfortable conditions. On the other hand we visited old, very cramped, and almost unbearably noisy factories which relied on quite primitive, labour intensive equipment. However, we were told that in general the textile shops in Shengze were far larger than elsewhere. And the trend in the local silk industry was towards a smaller number of larger enterprises. Consolidation had been fostered by funds provided by both the town and county level administrations. Some former town-run enterprises (e.g. the Xinlian, Xinfeng and Xinda factories) were transferred to the county many years earlier as part of a major restructuring programme. Such county-owned silk enterprises did not contribute much directly to the economy of Shengze, but their development had stimulated a rapid growth in locally-run facilities. The large financial reserves accumulated by the town - well over 1.2 billion yuan by the mid-1990s - would, we were informed, be targetted at accelerating the trend towards technologically more sophisticated and less labour intensive industrial processes. This was designed partly to increase the competitiveness of the local silk industry, but also to restrict the demand for labour and thereby address the problems, such as overcrowding and housing needs, which accompany an influx of labour.

The development of an off-farm economy in Shengze during the early reform period was based on collective ownership. Officials often drew a contrast between Shengze and towns in the nearby province of Zhejiang where private enterprise was the mainspring of economic reform. This collective approach to development came to be known in the early 1980s as the 'South Jiangsu Model'. Planning collectively enabled economies of scale in industry and allowed the local authorities to accumulate large financial reserves for investment. From their inception the township enterprises received nothing from the state and they operated according to the demands of the market. However, because so many of their employees came from the countryside, such enterprises had relatively low costs in terms of pension provision and welfare benefits such as hospital bills and nurseries.

We spoke to the deputy Party secretary of Shengze. He expressed great pride in the growth in the township enterprises, boasting that they were amongst the largest in China. He informed us that the official title of 'national big enterprises' had been awarded to the Wujiang Shengze Printing and Dyeing Mill, and also to the Wujiang Crafts Textiles Mill. Both had assets amounting to several hundred million yuan.

Silk has traditionally been traded as well as made in Shengze. In the late Ming and early Qing periods the silk market was located along the banks of the Shi river and it traded daily. More recently, following the interregnum of the planned economy period, when all products had to be exported through the State Foreign Trade Corporation, it was the opening of the Oriental Silk Market in 1986 that signalled Shengze's revival as an international centre for silk. This market, run by Wujiang city, had been expanded four times since it opened and was regarded as China's most important trading centre for real and artificial silk. Traders could now export directly, rather than through state channels, while information on the state of the silk market was provided by a special department within Wujiang city. The success of Shengze's silk market gave an enormous boost to the commercial and service sectors in Shengze, leading to the establishment of a wide range of service facilities, including banks, hotels, restaurants and transport. However, the expansion of the market had not kept pace with demand, resulting in a proliferation of predominantly silk retail outlets along Shengxin Road and Shengze Avenue. In response, another market - Oriental Silk City - had been established. This was a town-run enterprise, enabling Shengze to wrest a share of the benefits from Wujiang municipality with its Oriental Silk Market. The close relationship between silk manufacture and trade had led to Shengze becoming a thriving commercial and service centre. Many of the facilities, including several hotels, were operated by local silk concerns. In Shengze commerce

---

DEPUTY DIRECTOR OF THE TOWNSHIP INDUSTRY BUREAU OF WUJIANG MUNICIPALITY

Wujiang is a second tier city under which Shengze is governed.

As to whether economic development is more important than environmental protection, I think they go hand in hand. If pollution gets so serious as to be a health risk, it will be tackled. This is the way it happened in western countries: they first of all developed themselves, and then set about repairing the environmental damage, partly by exporting polluting industry to developing countries. For example, plastics, chemicals and vehicles are all polluting industries and they have been sent to China. Wherever industry develops there will be pollution. This is normal. If the machine is turned off, there'll be no noise. As soon as it's turned on there'll be noise. Unavoidable. For ourselves, we've developed a dyeing industry which causes serious water pollution. This should be tackled in due course. The officials say they're very keen to address the problem but in fact the worst thing is they just seem to ignore it. We're trying to stress a policy which considers pollution prevention as an integral part of the production process. But this doesn't prevent some enterprises just emphasising production. The main problem is that many factories are too small in scale to be able to afford pollution abatement. If an enterprise is losing money or unable to pay its workers, how could it afford to tackle pollution? This is a really complicated problem.

---

was more valuable than agriculture, which was still unusual for rural China. The shops in the town core stocked a range of goods similar to that found in much larger urban areas, and local residents - particularly the young - carried most of the internationally famous designer labels on their clothes.

While Shengze has long been associated overwhelmingly with the silk industry, other industrial activities had been established in the recent past. We visited an enterprise run by Changzhou village which was engaged in the manufacture of copper cable. The quoted cost of its establishment was 2.3 million yuan, none of which was provided by the state. It seemed most of the money came from a Canadian bank, probably as part of an aid package. This sophisticated operation was housed in a spacious set of buildings and used modern equipment imported from the United States, Switzerland and Finland, at a cost of nearly half a million dollars. Some of the copper used was imported, some came from within China. The profits from this concern, with the exception of an 'administrative fee' payable to Shengze *zhen*, and national and village land taxes, were retained at village level. Interestingly, the expertise required for the development of this enterprise was provided by retired workers and technicians from Shanghai who worked on a consultancy basis. Industrial links between Shengze and the major metropolitan areas, particularly Shanghai, were not confined to personnel: some enterprises were joint ventures, with certain processes being delegated to Shengze, while in other cases town and village-level enterprises would purchase used equipment from the major centres.

Environmental Issues

Natural Hazards

Shengze's low lying situation means that it is vulnerable to flooding during periods of intense rainfall, such as during typhoons, and when surface water levels are high due to excessive river discharge from elsewhere in the catchment. Local residents referred to at least a dozen serious floods during the 20th century, some of which were vividly recalled. The floods of 1983 and 1987 were particularly severe. In 1987, two thirds of the town area was submerged, in places to waist depth. During these periods the local economy was forced to suspend operations, causing large losses in revenue. In the winter of the same year, with the help of the (then) Wujiang county government, Shengze raised over eight million yuan for flood control projects. Four floodgates and 13 drainage stations were completed by the end of 1988. Since then the town has passed through the flood season safely.

Pollution

The rapid urbanisation and industrialisation of Shengze have inevitably resulted in changes in environmental quality. Although we have no biophysical data, the head of the town's construction and land administration office informed us that the quality of drinking water failed to meet the national standard. Local perceptions of water quality were addressed during the survey. None of the interviewed Shengze residents rated their drinking water as 'very good', while 16 per cent rated the water as poor. Furthermore, nearly a half of Shengze respondents perceived a recent change in taste in their drinking water. Changes in taste were probably associated with the introduction of water treatment in Shengze. Water quality was raised as an issue by many informants. A middle-aged women told us that as a small child she would wash clothes with her mother in the river in front of the house, but the water had become too polluted by the factories to wash anything, while domestic rubbish thrown into the waterways attracted flies and mosquitoes. A professional fortune teller who used water for divining purposes reported finding sediment in his storage jars. A local paediatrician was convinced that the high incidence of gastric infection among Shengze's children could be attributed to the water they drank, while adults, who were largely unaffected, may have become habituated. We encountered the local custom of swallowing a spoonful of vinegar before meals, apparently to neutralise the high levels of alkaline substances deposited into local water by printing and dyeing factories. The vinegar was taken specifically to prevent diarrhoea, which we were told was very common in the area. This was a statement we were able to confirm from experience. It seemed that some aspects of water quality, specifically those associated with untreated sewage disposal, had been greatly improved by water treatment. However, conventional water treatment would have little effect on the cocktail of chemical substances which were being discharged in increasing amounts. It appeared that one set of pollution problems had been replaced by another.

Shengze's pollution problems became national news in 1994 after a major fish kill near the town of Jiaxing in neighbouring Zhejiang province. The Jiaxing authorities attributed the fish deaths to discharges from the dyeing factories in Shengze. This was not the first time that the Jiaxing authorities had complained to Shengze about pollution, but this time they reported the case to the Zhejiang government, which in turn reported it to the National People's Congress. Shengze's official response was that the high fish mortality was due to abnormally hot weather which had reduced water flow (and presumably lowered oxygen concentration in the water). Furthermore, the town of Jiaxing also had printing and dyeing works, and a paper factory, all of which discharged untreated water. It was thus impossible to attribute the cause of the fish kill with any certainty. However, this inter-town altercation received wide publicity, promoted by coverage on national television. Our discussions with local residents, combined with our own observations, provided strong evidence of a major water pollution problem in Shengze. Certainly, all the surface water we saw was murky. In some places it was red or dark blue, clear evidence of discharges from the local dyeing industry.

The response to our question about air quality was broadly similar to that for water quality. Only seven per cent of Shengze respondents rated air quality as 'very fresh' and 20 per cent categorised air quality as 'poor' or 'very poor'. Also, over a quarter of those we interviewed believed there had been recent changes in air quality. Despite this perception of declining air quality standards, however, two-thirds of Shengze's respondents still rated air quality as 'fresh'. Only 35 per cent of Shengze respondents wanted additional polluting industries in the town, even with the compensation of higher incomes, and only 18 per cent expressed a willingness to take hazardous work.

One of our key informants on environmental issues was the chief of the environmental protection bureau in Wujiang city. He was originally trained as a teacher but later entered Jiangsu's Party College. After working as a town head for five years he was assigned to Wujiang in 1993 to take charge of environmental protection. His unit had a staff of 43 professionals, many of them college trained, plus a number of administrators. The bureau had two divisions, one for monitoring and the other for supervisory work. His staff investigated environmental problems, collected fees, imposed fines and dealt with complaints. The work of the bureau was principally funded by the enterprises, which supplied about five million yuan annually. Ten per cent of the money raised was passed on to the provincial authorities, 10-20 per cent was needed for the bureau's work while the remainder was said to be handed back to the enterprises to improve environmental protection facilities. The bureau clearly had major problems with the volume of work arising from rapid industrialisation and urbanisation in the region. Some small towns, designated in the 1990s had not long since been small villages, while already established centres, such as Shengze, had greatly expanded with the development of industry and influx of workers. Despite the difficulties, our informant emphasised the new importance of environmental protection in Wujiang city. He singled out Shengze for special consideration because of the major water pollution problems created by the printing and dyeing industry, and the various chemical plants. He cited the problem of local fish tasting of oil. He characterised Shengze's approach as 'develop first, improve later', which he believed was 'the inevitable road of the underdeveloped country'. Certainly, this philosophy was confirmed in our discussions with Shengze's deputy governor. However, the environmental bureau chief declared that his own preference was to deal with the environmental issues from the outset. 'Economic growth is meaningless without protection for the environment', he told us. Despite such rhetoric, however, he was clearly pragmatic in his work. For example, he was mindful that the downturn in the local economy (mid-1990s) meant that it was impracticable for existing TVEs to install pollution protection equipment.

However, new projects did have to be approved on environmental grounds. The main issue for his department was the older factories which were built and equipped in the 1970s without regard to emissions. He informed us that in the last few years heavy fines had been imposed on some enterprises, and some had been ordered to stop production. In cases of non-compliance the perpetrators had been taken to court. However he also admitted that pollution issues were largely left to the 'environmental consciousness' of the management, and acknowledged that some enterprises operated their pollution controls only when an inspection was known to be imminent. He believed greater attention needed to be paid to the training of enterprise managers in order to emphasise the importance of pollution control. He also informed us of the major problem created by the disposal of domestic rubbish and the discharge of sewage into local water courses, both of which were conspicuous. The town was in the process of establishing a large land-fill site to deal with the former problem.

Land Loss

The recent conversion of good agricultural land for residential, infrastructural, industrial and commercial purposes was very conspicuous in Shengze. The figure quoted to us was that one-sixth of agricultural land had been lost to such developments since the early 1980s. Our key informant on land issues in Shengze was the director of the construction office and land management bureau. He came from a local peasant family and until he was 29 years old worked as a political instructor in the army. On demobilisation he was allocated a job in Shengze where he administered the emigration of high school graduates to the villages. He joined the construction office in 1982. His office had jurisdiction over the whole *zhen*. Essentially he had responsibility for three areas of work, town development, other general construction, and land administration. There were two deputy directors in each of the two construction offices and another in the land administration office. He informed us that most of his staff members were educated to high school level, or above, and their average age was 45 years. As overall head of the organisation his most difficult job, and one that took a quarter of his time, was to reconcile conflicts between the construction departments and the land administration. The land problem was particularly acute in Shengze because of the number of wealthy residents seeking to build new houses and because the *zhen* was not well endowed with land. A huge problem for the land administration office was their lack of enforcement powers. If someone built a house without permission, we were told, the office of land administration could not directly intervene, but had to petition the court, a time consuming and expensive route. Therefore each case required special mediation. In addition there were other considerations that needed to be taken into account with individual cases. Our informant cited the case of a taxation officer who built a new house. He refused to stop building or to demolish the part already built, although instructed to do so by the land administration office. The local authorities were powerless because the transgressor, in his official role, exercised a great deal of influence over the scale of revenues raised for the town's coffers. He also commanded relationships with potential investors.

Another major problem was to find the land needed for the many development projects which the town was undertaking, such as a new craft weaving mill which was planned to occupy 65 hectares. To acquire land for a particular project the construction office applied to the town's Industry, Agriculture and Commerce Holding Company. If there was general agreement that the proposal fitted the development plan for the town the organisation involved would be asked to submit a formal application. This had to include details concerning the supply of electricity and water and vehicular access to the site. The construction office was empowered to issue licences for developments occupying up to three mu of land; applications for land areas between three and 15 mu required the consent of the authorities in Suzhou city, while areas in excess of 15 mu were submitted to the provincial authorities. The chief of the construction and land administration office stated that regulations would be much easier to implement if recourse to the courts, to mediation and to law enforcement was more straightforward. He told us this was the situation in the provinces of Henan and Sichuan. Apparently land administration officers in Shengze had previously worn uniforms but this practice was now forbidden.

Planning Issues

A degree of physical planning was evident in Shengze, and was expressed most conspicuously in the emphasis placed on zoning. New residential areas lay to the west of the town core, along with commercial and trading enterprises, while the main industrial area was situated to the east. The town's deputy head and deputy Party secretary was enthusiastic about planning but he believed most people did not take it seriously. This included the enterprise officials who were, he said, only interested in profit. He was particularly concerned that an increasingly market orientated economy would further weaken the planning process in Shengze because economic imperatives would determine land allocation and use. He gave us the example of an old town resident who opened a shop without permission, and despite protests from neighbours. When told by the town government to close down the business, the new shopkeeper simply shut the premises for two days and then reopened without protest from neighbours. Financial inducements to neighbours appear to have resolved the issue. Another example was provided by the recently retired deputy director of the town's construction office. In 1994 the town had taken over some land for development, but because of a downturn in the local economy in the mid-1990s they were unable to proceed. To raise some money the land was leased to various private enterprises. Now the land was occupied by banks, hotels, karaoke bars, restaurants, shops, and dance halls, without any planning, and there had been much complaint from the ordinary residents who could not afford to partake of any of these services. The town's deputy head enumerated a number of problems which prevented the implementation of proper planning procedures in Shengze. Most important was the lack of a legal framework specifically for the administration of small towns. There was also the shortage of appropriately trained personnel: we came across no-one with any college-level planning qualifications. A further problem for Shengze was that the county-level enterprises fell outside the town's jurisdiction.

Living in Shengze

Transport and Communications

The secretary of the Party branch of Shengze's transportation section provided an overview of transportation in the town. His office was responsible for registering and taxing motor vehicles. The town's first motor vehicle was obtained as late as 1974, by one of the silk factories, but in the 1980s and 1990s the number of vehicles had grown steadily. There were now nearly 1,000 vehicles registered in the town, and some 10,000 motorcycles. The growth in road traffic had been responsible for a decline in water transport: in the 1970s there were 200-300 boats in the locality but now water transport had practically ceased. Regional coach services began in the 1980s, provided by the state-owned Wujiang Travel Company, and Shengze was well connected by a fleet of 150 buses to other towns and cities. For example, there were frequent services between Shengze and the cities of Shanghai and Suzhou as well as to various locations in and around Wujiang. Local transport was provided mainly by pedicabs and to a lesser extent by minibuses. The pedicabs, many of which were operated by migrants, were difficult to regulate, and some were not officially licensed. In 1994 there was a major campaign to identify the unlicensed operators which led to many being ordered out of service. In a bid to reduce the number of pedicabs on the streets, operators were supposed to work only on alternate days. A set fee (five yuan in 1996) was charged for transport in the town core while rates were negotiable for longer journeys.

Travel around and through Shengze had been greatly improved by a new ring road system, but access to the town core area was confined to just one thoroughfare, Shengxin Road. A representative from Shengze's Traffic and Transportation Management Institute told us that each day a massive 80,000-90,000 vehicle trips could be counted on this road. Unsurprisingly, major traffic jams were a feature of Shengze's town-core area, a problem that was exacerbated by the narrow streets. Many of our key informants, as well as those we interviewed in our household survey, made reference to the growing chaos in the town-core area. The growth of traffic, and general congestion, in the town core clearly presented the local administration with a formidable challenge.

The town's telephone system was installed in the 1970s. By the mid-1990s at least one in seven households had its own telephone, including some rural households. The town had enough installed capacity for 13,000 lines and was planning another 5,000. The development of a stratum of wealthy business people had also resulted in a large increase in the number of pagers and mobile phones used locally.

Housing

Most residents of Shengze's town core occupied public housing, constructed from the 1960s onwards. Those built in the 1960s and 1970s tended to have small sitting rooms, kitchens and bathrooms but relatively large bedrooms. Those built from the 1980s onwards reversed this arrangement. Local people, accustomed to a highly collectivised environment, seemed to find this form of accommodation congenial. Some residents still lived in 'old Shengze', a cluster of narrow, winding lanes and traditional houses found along the south side of Shengze Avenue. Here, alleyways too narrow for two bicycles to pass thread past anonymous entries. Behind them were modest courtyards leading to dilapidated, two-storey homes still bearing signs of the lush paintwork applied by distant inhabitants. Some residents came by these properties through inheritance; others had them assigned by their work units. Most of these old houses were now occupied by several families, often related, and were subdivided accordingly. The old guest halls had often been preserved as communal kitchens or living spaces. Many of these houses gave directly on to streams and rivers, 'Venetian style'. Formerly, the residents washed themselves, their clothing and their vegetables in the adjacent water courses. These practices have virtually ceased, although we did see people deposit waste water into the rivers.

Many buildings in the business streets combined a retail outlet with accommodation above the shop. Families living here typically confined themselves to a few cramped rooms on the upper floor in order to maximise the space for the business. Hygiene facilities in the old town were perfunctory and most residents used public toilets or the commodes that were still common within the houses, placed in a discreet corner and screened by a sheet. Pressure of space in the old town meant that furnishings were basic and practical. The residents of public housing projects did rather better, and younger tenants prided themselves on a full array of consumer durables and modern, self-assembly furniture.

As elsewhere, in the countryside people were responsible for their own housing. Many had used their newly acquired savings to build new properties. These were usually either two- or three-storey family houses, often quite substantial by traditional standards. The interiors of older properties, once used as storage for grain and agricultural implements, were now occupied by white goods and consumer electronics. We visited an opulent example of the new kind of dwelling, owned by a newly wealthy family. It was built in the style of a European villa at, it was repeatedly claimed, a cost of several hundred thousand yuan. The ground floor of this three-storey home contained two sitting rooms, a bathroom and a very large kitchen. The centre of the house had been made into an atrium, open to the ceiling of the third floor from which a crystal chandelier descended to the ground floor. Under it a miniature indoor garden had been built. A spiral staircase snaked upwards past the children's rooms on the first floor to the master bedroom on the second, which was also endowed with a large balcony. There was a bathroom on every floor, complete with a flush toilet. It was a style apparently copied from that of luxury hotels and represented the summit of local aspirations. Lower down the income scale, people in the countryside tended to live in roomy, two-storey dwellings with an open plan kitchen, living and dining area on the ground floor and bedrooms above. These houses were typically well stocked with self-assembly furniture and consumer appliances, but the families had not included bathrooms when they had originally built the properties and so relied on commodes. These dwellings housed the local equivalent of the aspiring middle class.

Waste Disposal

Over 60 per cent of households in the survey were connected to sewers. This included most of the houses in the town core. In the countryside, however, sewerage existed only in newly built houses. From most rural homes with a flush toilet the waste was simply piped to the nearest convenient water course. Those without sewerage connections deposited their waste either into a public drain, a cesspool, or the river. River disposal was still very common in the countryside although it also occurred in the town-core area. Little of the industrial waste water was treated: most was discharged directly to water courses.

Population growth and growing prosperity had led to an increasing amount of solid waste, and disposal methods varied. Some of our respondents simply threw their rubbish out into the street or on to the nearest convenient patch of waste ground or dry river bed. Signs of fly tipping were very apparent around the town. Each vacant lot seemed to attract its quota of rubbish, which in turn attracted flies and mosquitoes, creating a health hazard. Other residents used public bins, or bagged their rubbish for removal, a practice promoted on the newer public housing estates. These neighbourhoods were conspicuously cleaner than the older districts as a result. Garbage was removed to four public dumps for disposal and treatment.

However, over 80 per cent of households in our survey claimed they were satisfied with the waste disposal methods used. Those that were dissatisfied often commented that people had not changed their ideas to conform with the town's new-found prosperity, probably because they had no conception of public hygiene or their responsibility to others. Some respondents blamed migrant workers, said to have poor hygiene and dirty habits, for the increased burden of rubbish in the town. Not only had the total waste burden increased in recent years but a shift had occurred in its composition. Cursory inspection of domestic consumption patterns revealed a trend towards lower biodegradability of by-products as plastics and metals replaced naturally-based materials. This shift was recognised by our respondents in Shengze. Forty per cent of them claimed that the composition of their domestic rubbish had changed in recent years. It was clear that the public facilities provided for waste disposal were inadequate in Shengze. However, the responsibility could not be placed solely on the local authorities and nor could it be deflected on to migrants. Much more cooperation was obviously needed on the part of Shengze citizens if the situation was to improve.

Fuels

Every one of the households in our survey was connected to the electricity supply. It was our understanding that this situation pertained for all officially registered households in Shengze. Refrigerators and air conditioning units had become extremely common, a trend which was probably encouraged by a succession of very hot summers in the early 1990s. The very large increase in both domestic and industrial electricity demand during this decade put strains on the electricity supply system. Despite the installation of extra generating power, cuts were a fact of life and occurred during our visits. Nearly 80 per cent of surveyed households used gas for cooking. The gas was piped or bottled. According to one of our respondents, who worked in a village women's association, bottled gas was formerly saved for festival days, while rice straw was the common fuel at other times in Shengze. With rising incomes and changes in lifestyle, rice straw was now used only by families still working the land.

Food and Drink

As a typical 'water town' of the lower Yangzi plain, Shengze's staple food, was rice. An exception to this generalisation was that the migrants from northern and western parts of China favoured foods based on wheat flour as dietary staples. We found that local people were very discriminating in their food consumption habits. And they had a lot to choose between. We routinely counted over 30 different kinds of vegetables in the market. Residents were well supplied not only with favourites like pork and chicken but also with comparatively exotic fare, such as rabbit. However, Shengze remained predominantly a town of 'fish and rice' and people still

---

DIRECTOR OF SHENGZE'S NEW HOSPITAL

Shengze has built itself a large, well-equipped, hospital with several dozen doctors, many of them specialised.

Now the economy is developing, the demands of the patients vary. Some come in ambulances which we heavily subsidise. Some come in pedicabs, and for this they have to pay a little more. Others come in their luxury limousines. Our own staff can deal with the ordinary patients. For those who demand a better service, specialists are available. In fact we have about 30 we can call on. For those who insist on something even better, we get doctors from some of the best hospitals in Suzhou and even Shanghai. Many are well-known professors.

Those who demand a superior service fall into two groups. First, the managers of various state and collective organisations. Secondly, there are the self-employed and private sector business people. Our charges are according to state regulations and in 1995 we raised about five million yuan from them. The hospital is OK for ordinary people but not for managers and entrepreneurs. They're busy most of the time and their state of mind is important. They only tend to stop working if they're really ill. They can't work in a ward full of patients. So we're planning to build a new convalescence wing here so that the managers can stay in single or double rooms with air-conditioning and telephones.

---

favoured a local cuisine that emphasised freshwater fish and other aquatic products, including shrimp and soft shelled crabs. Interviewees told us they used to fish for their own food from the local rivers and lakes, but many watercourses were now filled in or no longer provided significant catches of fish. Accordingly, supplies now came from the market. Traditional preferences were also maintained in the form of tea drinking, which in some cases consumed a substantial proportion of the local food budget. Tea was made in a distinctive local style which sometimes involved the addition of beansprouts and white sesame seeds.

While traditional dietary practices were still maintained, prosperity had brought with it both an increasing concern with taste and nutrition and an openness to unfamiliar foods, including eggs, milk and, especially, fruit. The diet had diversified to the extent that local people were now familiar with foreign convenience foods. While visiting local shopping malls we saw a promotion for an American brand of instant coffee, complete with bunting, banners and various gaudy point-of-sale devices. Just a few years ago such a display would have drawn fascinated crowds in Shengze; now it formed part of everyday life.

In the 1960s, nearly all of the water drunk in Shengze was drawn from rivers, lakes and wells. By the early 1990s, however, nearly all households had a piped water supply. Indeed, none of the many households we visited relied on local well or surface water supplies, although a few used such sources for some purposes. Industrial development and population growth had put enormous pressure on the water supply and we were told by the manager of the waterworks that preparations were underway to expand capacity from 35,000 to 50,000 tonnes per day. This would be sufficient to meet peak demand from industry, which consumed seven litres for every three consumed domestically. Concerns were expressed, however, about the progressive decline in water quality from the source area, which is Xibaiyang lake to the west of Shengze. It is of course well known that lakes in the industrialised parts of southern and eastern China are often highly polluted with a cocktail of substances, many of which are not removed by conventional water treatment facilities. A doctor we spoke to was convinced that water quality had already declined despite the installation of water treatment equipment and a piped supply.

Health and Welfare

The Shengze Hospital, formerly Shengze Commune Hospital, was built in 1955 and served both the town and area of the former county. In its earlier days the hospital was a fairly basic clinic which as late as 1984 employed only one qualified doctor. Since then expansion had been impressive. Five million yuan was raised in 1986 for improving facilities and the purchase of new equipment, and our visit coincided with a drive to raise a further one million yuan for another expansion in services. By the mid-1990s the hospital dealt with over 260,000 cases a year and 94 per cent of the hospital's 200 beds were occupied at any one time. A wide range of clinical and surgical treatments was carried out, including colon and breast cancer operations. Some surgical procedures carried out at the hospital were videotaped for educational purposes. There were 48 supervisory level doctors and each year a dozen or so medical school graduates were employed. Retired specialists from larger hospitals also served as honorary directors and played an important role in maintaining clinical standards and hosting seminars on advanced and specialised clinical practices. Close links were maintained with larger hospitals in Suzhou and Shanghai, which provided training and specialised clinical services. The rapid upgrading of services provided by the hospital had the effect of increasing the numbers of patients. We were told, however, that the hospital was satisfactory for 'ordinary people', but not 'managers and entrepreneurs'. Accordingly, a recovery room for the latter was nearing completion, fitted with single and double rooms, air conditioning and telephones. The rationale for this development, we were told, was that business people did not like to sacrifice working time while recovering from medical treatment.

Cooperative medical care still existed in Shengze, under the supervision of the local Medical Management Association (*yiliao guanli hui*). Provision took the form of a joint medical insurance programme, to which individuals, the local authority and township enterprises all contributed. Medical bills for less than a few hundred yuan were borne by the patient, but for those who were eligible, more expensive treatments could be subsidised by the health insurance programme on a progressive sliding scale.

We learned from hospital doctors and some local residents that 'snail fever' (schistosomiasis) was once widespread locally: hospital records showed that around 2000 people suffered from this condition as recently as the 1970s. This disease had been officially eliminated, but the numbers of gastroenteritis and, very worryingly, typhoid cases were increasing. Doctors attributed the former to changing diets and the latter to declining water quality. Medical staff who had transferred to Shengze from other regions informed us that the incidence of typhoid was greater than elsewhere. We were told that the incidence of lung cancer and heart disease was also rising, both of which are diseases of urban lifestyles and affluence.

Public Security

Our principal informant on policing and security issues was the Party representative at Shengze police station. There were eight 'guarding stations' in Shengze, and the town was allocated a quota of 57 officers, although an additional 23 officers were employed. Many of the police had a senior middle school education, and some had attended police college. We were told there was a shortage of money for policing, and an undisclosed proportion of the police budget was raised by fines. We were quoted standard fines of 3,000 yuan for gambling and 5,000 yuan for prostitution. The average salary for a policeman was quite low for Shengze, at around 5,500 yuan a year. In addition to the town police force, individual factories usually had their own 'militia' to patrol the premises while smaller enterprises tended to hire guards from security companies.

All those we spoke to on the issues of security and public order told us local crime had increased markedly in the past few years, and that migrant labour was primarily responsible. Apparently, in 1992 around 70 per cent of Shengze's crime had been committed by incomers, but due to tighter security this proportion had subsequently declined. It was asserted that the crime rate increased when building workers were laid off during extended periods of rain. Concern about the increasing crime-wave in Shengze was evidenced by various counter measures that had been introduced. First, residents were recruited to supplement regular police patrols. Some 150 civilians worked with the police in this way in the town core, with a further 250 residents in the rural areas. Second, over 40 retirees had been recruited to keep watch in residential areas. Third, what might be called a rapid response team was established in 1994. It had around 20 members and three vehicles and could be accessed by an emergency telephone number. Despite these innovations, a young paediatrician told us she would not go out unaccompanied at night in Shengze.

Education

The town was served educationally by three high schools, all of which had been renovated in recent years. The oldest, Shengze High School, was established in the 1940s. This school had recently undergone a major rebuilding programme which included a new library, laboratories and accommodation for boarders. Shengze Silk College, located near the Oriental Silk Market, served as a vocational institute. It took middle school graduates from Shengze town and taught them production technologies and craft skills. This college served as the major source of skilled labour for local industry. Among our respondents, about 10 percent had never attended school and a further 40 per cent of respondents had only a primary education. Only 15 per cent had been to higher middle school and five per cent had been to college.

Leisure, Customs and Religion

In terms of lifestyle and aspirations of Shengze residents, the proximity to Shanghai - a city of immense political, economic and cultural weight - must have been of immense significance. In addition, Shengze has long had links with a wider world because of the international nature of the silk trade. Our assessment at the close of the 20th century was that Shengze was a city in miniature with a cosmopolitan outlook, advanced ideas and an appreciation of media and technology. Residents were increasingly linked to the world by cable television, and to each other by their mobile phones, sported ostentatiously in the streets.

One of the characteristics of modern societies is the migration of leisure activities from public to private spaces. This was becoming evident in Shengze. The cinema on Shenxing Road was frequented almost entirely by migrants. Local people preferred the intimacy of the karaoke bars or viewed the world through the private window of the 10 regional television stations. Ninety-eight per cent of the surveyed households contained a television set and three quarters of them said they watched for two hours or more per day. Viewing habits varied by age and occupation. Older people preferred transmissions of traditional *yueju* and *pingtan* operas. Businessmen, in contrast, made a point of watching national and international news in keeping with their self-image. Younger people preferred a diet of international news and Western soap operas. Ninety per cent of households had a radio. Sixty-two per cent of respondents claimed they regularly read magazines and/or newspapers. Business magazines were particularly popular amongst the young business-orientated residents.

Although the influence of modernity was everywhere apparent in Shengze, recent times had also seen a rebirth of traditional customs and practices, especially those associated with religion. Shengze has a long religious history. The town's famous Yuanming temple and the Daoist *zheng* palace were built during the Song dynasty. In the Yuan dynasty (1279-1378), the Buddhist monk Shanyin founded the Yuanzhao monastery. By the end of the Qing, Shengze had become a local centre for Christian belief, both Protestant and Catholic. Religious places and practices, at least in public, were largely eliminated during the Cultural Revolution, but have subsequently revived considerably. During our time in Shengze, we witnessed the inauguration of a very large new 'Three-selfs' church in one of the older sections of the town. Since the 1980s there had been a revival of some of the old customs, for example the worship of the deity Zhao, widely practiced by older people in the countryside. In keeping with the town's business traditions, the festival of worshipping the god of wealth between the 1st and 4th day of the Chinese New Year remained particularly popular. Each year at this time the spirit of enterprise was promoted with a display of firecrackers.

The wider culture of Shengze was clearly considerably influenced by its proximity to Suzhou and to Zhejiang province. But the town also displayed some unique customs drawn from its silk producing heritage. When the industry was booming during the Qing dynasty, the local unemployed would wait by the town's bridges to be selected for casual labour in the mills. This ritual of 'walking the bridge' was still recalled as a local ceremony. March and April were also traditionally the 'silkworm months' and saw the staging of the 'silkworm shutting the door' (*chan guan men*) ceremony. This would be inaugurated with a procession of farmers to the local temples where prayers were offered for a good harvest. The town would then effectively shut down. Funerals, weddings and other celebrations ceased and tax gathering was suspended. Each family stayed at home behind a front door 'sealed' by a sheet of red paper. This period would end with a three day public holiday, enlivened by theatrical troupes hired by the local trade associations to play at the Silk Temple. This building still stood, but was used as a warehouse.

Despite the vogue for karaoke lounges, tea houses still performed an important social function in Shengze. Once ubiquitous across the town, they played very much the same role in the local economy as the Restoration era coffee houses in the development of the financial sector in London. Traditionally, after business, people would retire to the tea houses to talk, settle disputes, make informal deals and listen to professional storytellers. The tea houses still existed, although the storytellers were replaced by cable feeds delivering news of international markets.

Wedding and funeral customs in Shengze demonstrated the influence of the modern era. Economic prosperity had encouraged rather than inhibited the traditional ostentation of wedding ceremonies. Formal engagement was followed by a succession of banquets, drinking parties, and the presentation of cash gifts, both for the engagement and the dowry proper. Dowries were especially lavish, and unlike many other places, were provided for by the labour of the bride herself. Many young women began saving for their dowry immediately on starting work. A large dowry demonstrated to the husband's family that their new member was capable, hard working and worthy of respect: it appeared to be an investment in status rather than a form of debt bondage. On death, cremation had become very common. The old customs like burning paper money had become rare. At the cremation ceremony, family members would wear mourning dress while other guests would mark the occasion with black, silk armbands. After the ceremony, the family usually provided a vegetarian banquet for the guests.

Future Developments

We have remarked earlier that the metamorphosis of Shengze's town core into a completely modern small town (*sensu lato*) would be virtually complete by the first few years of the 21st century. What we meant here is that all those infrastructure features which are taken for granted in the West - hospitals, schools, roads, modern transport, telecommunications, sewerage, water treatment - would be in place, and importantly, be reliable and efficient. Enormous changes have occurred in Shengze since the early 1980s; indeed this *zhen* represents well the dramatic transformation of lives and landscapes that has occurred in eastern and southern China since the early 1980s. As such, the town is also a microcosm for the problems faced by such fast-developing centres. The high concentration of people and vehicles in the town core was already a major problem: it was immediately obvious during our visits and was remarked upon by many of the surveyed residents as well as by the key informants representing the town leadership and the various official departments. Separation of people and vehicles had already been attempted to a limited extent and there were plans to pursue such an arrangement where possible in the future. The completion of the ring road will speed traffic flow around the town, although the growth in traffic will inevitably negate the benefits to some extent. A more pressing problem for resolution is the accommodation of the large projected increase of vehicles in the town core with its one main thoroughfare and network of narrow roads and alleyways. There were plans to clear away the older, high density residences which may go some way to alleviate this problem in a physical sense but the social problems associated with such development did not appear to feature prominently in the various schemes.

We were told repeatedly that money was short for infrastructural developments. In fact all the key informants in administrative roles mentioned the lack of capital for investment as the chief problem for the town. Hundreds of million yuan are required for the various infrastructural projects now underway or projected. Yet the town received just one million yuan per year from the government. One way to raise money was to lease land for new development. For example, when money was required to complete the south circular road, blocks of land close to the road were auctioned to individuals or enterprises. Another method was to lease land in the development zones, of which there were three, covering about 30 hectares. When the development zones were built they were served with electricity, water and road facilities. It was quicker, and much more profitable, to sell the land directly to individuals rather than construct new houses which conformed to a particular design. This was still a novel approach locally, but it was clear that the authorities intended to pursue it increasingly in the future. While such developments have advantages in terms of profitability, however, they also limit the extent to which the local authorities can exercise control over the nature of the developments. The deputy director of Wujiang city's township industrial bureau complained that despite the fact that his organisation was supposed to be in charge of enterprise development it had rather lost its purpose and its powers were certainly decreasing. It seemed that township enterprises, particularly the larger ones, simply by-passed his office and dealt directly with other organisations, most notably the banks. This trend will sharpen in the future, with important implications for environmental protection and planning.

The pattern of residential accommodation is set to change. First, the older houses in the old town are to be cleared away and replaced by apartment blocks. Second, demand for European-style villa residences is increasing among the more wealthy residents. There were already indications that the latter style of living was the one to aspire to. Such developments, which have created western-style suburbs around the main urban centres in China will inevitably occupy more and more cultivable land and become a more conspicuous feature in the predominantly agricultural hinterland of the town core. The notion of separate town core and rural elements in the *zhen* will look increasingly vulnerable. Increased demand for such housing will be complemented by the demand for further industrial developments, particularly in the villages because industrialisation was seen as the only path to increased wealth. We have no doubt that Shengze *zhen* will develop in this way, and develop very quickly. With such a scenario it is difficult to believe that claims made by the *zhen* leadership for agricultural self-sufficiency in the 1990s will have much credence in 2010.

Having achieved such rapid economic development, most Shengze residents no longer worried unduly about necessities such as food, clothing, and work. We detected a developing interest in cuisine, fashion, and opportunities for personal development. Lifestyles would be increasingly influenced by the major metropolitan centres, not only in China, but internationally. Shengze's Party secretary captured the prevailing spirit, if somewhat whimsically, and pointed to the future when he told us:

> Our target is to wave good-bye to affluence and march towards modernisation. We want to build full-scale agribusiness and modern enterprises serving global markets. We want to make Shengze's environment beautiful. To achieve all this, Shengze's people will face many new problems and challenges. But the future is so alluring that we are happy to make the effort.

5 Concluding Remarks

Our objective in writing this book was to use our archive of information, data and experience in an attempt to capture a sense of place, and a sense of mood, in just three Chinese small towns in the last few years of the 20th century. So much of the published work on small towns concentrates on economic issues, frequently using aggregated data, or else details the 'official position', but it is more difficult to conceive of how such *zhen* operate, how they are organised, and what it is like to live in such a place - in short, what actually happens on the ground. As we say in our preface, no claims are made that our findings can be extrapolated without qualification - there are after all some 20,000 *zhen* in China - but similar set of questions could be appropriately asked in any one of them, and no doubt a similar suite of issues would be seen to be relevant. Moreover we have hoped to capture something of the enormous variation in socioeconomic development (so closely correlated with region) in small towns across China.

In this concluding chapter we want to draw together some of the major themes and data presented in the three *zhen* profiles, to place these in a comparative context, but also to point to features and problems which are shared by these *zhen*, and arguably by small town China generally despite enormous differences between *zhen* in geographical and socioeconomic context. First, it is important to restate that the changes experienced by each of the three *zhen* have to a varying extent been the product of the reforming policies instigated in the early 1980s. Of immense significance was the relaxation of government control over agricultural production - through the introduction of household responsibility systems - which raised the productivity of the rural labour force and provided a huge pool of labour for non-agricultural activities. Subsequent legislative changes in areas such as household registration, food rationing, urban employment, housing and welfare provision further lowered the obstacles to urbanisation in rural areas and assisted the inter-regional and inter-occupational movement of labour. Rural reforms were particularly important for Neiguan and Yuantan where they liberated the labour force from '*yi liang wei gang*' (grain is the key). In Shengze, however, the establishment of township industries had preceded the implementation of the household responsibility to some extent. The changes initiated by the reforms of the 1980s resulted not only in a huge change in the appearance of the Chinese countryside and myriad small rural towns, but also a sea-change in the outlook among inhabitants. Former notions of self-sufficiency and patriarch rule have been substantially replaced by a more adventurous and entrepreneurial spirit. And very significantly these changes have also led to the release from poverty of hundreds of millions of rural residents in a remarkably short time.

The marked contrast in the extent to which our *zhen* have experienced industrialisation and urbanisation was reflected in the employment profiles of those interviewed in our main survey. We deliberately selected around 30 per cent of respondents from outside the town-core areas in each of the three *zhen*. Yet while nearly 60 per cent of all respondents in Neiguan and Yuantan claimed to be peasants, less than one per cent of our sample of Shengze residents categorised themselves in this way. Correspondingly, while only 20 per cent of Shengze residents had their own grain supply, the equivalent figures for Neiguan and Yuantan were, respectively, 77 and 88 per cent. In Shengze only a small minority of local residents were engaged in farm work, and it was certainly not the work to which most local residents aspired. Most of the farm work was carried out by teams of contract workers, and more casual labour, imported from less developed regions. Income data also separate the three *zhen* along an axis of development. When respondents in each *zhen* were divided into approximately equal-sized groups on the basis of personal income, the mid income bands were 1000-2088 yuan in Neiguan, 1500-3000 yuan in Yuantan, and 4200-7000 yuan in Shengze. Even allowing for purchasing power disparities between regions, the trend in personal affluence was marked.

In all locations a frenzy of industrial activity had occurred during the reform period, and in Neiguan and Yuantan in particular, it started from a very low base. The TVE sector had from the outset adopted a market-orientated outlook and philosophy which has given it a considerable advantage over the less flexible urban enterprises. In fact it is not an exaggeration to claim that the 'socialist market economy' was conceptualised in the TVE sector. However it will be clear from the *zhen* profile chapters that this has not been an unqualified success. The total number of new enterprises exceeded by far those that remained by the mid-1990s. And at the time of our visit the viability of many of the survivors remained highly questionable. Even Shengze, reputedly among the wealthiest of Chinese *zhen*, is not immune from economic realities: it was clear that the silk industry was in the doldrums during the period of our study. The problems faced by TVEs at various stages of development were clearly in evidence in our chosen *zhen*. For Neiguan the major concern was how to attract and develop new projects appropriate to its very limited natural resources, with limited water supply being a key factor. A major problem for Yuantan was how to develop its existing industries in order to raise the value of their products, a process that will require an investment of both technology and skilled personnel. Similar problems of kind were evident in Shengze, but here the level of skills and technology already available were much more advanced than in Yuantan and the requirement was to match the highest international standards. In all three *zhen* the shortage of funds was bemoaned by the leaders we questioned, and it was reflected in inadequate infrastructures.

During our questionnaire survey we enquired about satisfaction with both income and living conditions in two simple questions in which respondents could select 'satisfied', 'not satisfied' or 'so-so' as responses. Dissatisfaction appeared to be much greater in the two less developed *zhen* (approximately 50 per cent for income and 40 per cent for living conditions) than in Shengze (only 18 per cent). However, the proportion of 'satisfied' respondents was no greater in the most advanced *zhen* than elsewhere. Shengze respondents were differentiated from those in the other two *zhen* by the significant proportion who equivocated (34 per cent compared with two per cent elsewhere): they could not reasonably complain of their current circumstances, but they were sufficiently familiar with consumer culture to appreciate that an entirely satisfactory standard of living had yet to be achieved.

Migration is an issue of huge social and economic significance in modern China, and we describe different facets of the phenomenon in each of the *zhen* profile chapters. Prominent in Neiguan was the out-migration, often to other provinces, of men of working age because of the limited opportunities for off-farm work locally and the shortage of agricultural land. It was therefore left for the women to provide much of the manual labour on the farms, including the very strenuous activity of terrace building and repair in the loess hills. Other movements were more local: women, predominantly, moved from countryside to the town core for work or marriage, or Neiguan residents moved to the county town of Dingxi for work during the week. Out-migration of males of working age to the cities of the coastal provinces was a feature of Yuantan's population movements, and as in Neiguan it meant that women were left with the responsibility of raising the child or children, taking care of family responsibilities and probably also carrying out farm work. The return of migrants to their home *zhen*, perhaps once a year for Spring Festival, had no doubt been a catalyst for change in perceptions and aspirations in this *zhen*. Yuantan's town core also received many in-migrants to work in the various township enterprises, but in addition, this *zhen* had a significant turnover of temporary residents en route for elsewhere because of the *zhen*'s position at the intersection of two major highways. In Shengze, in contrast to the other two locations, population movement was dominated by in-migration. While the official estimates put the proportion of migrants as a third of the total population, some believed the figure to be much higher. It was the newcomers who did most of the manual work, whether as factory operatives, as farm workers or as construction labourers. And in Neiguan, as elsewhere, it was the newcomers who were widely believed to be responsible for recent increases in crime.

The provision of most services and utilities was much more advanced in Shengze than elsewhere. Waste disposal was rudimentary in Neiguan and Yuantan, and certainly inadequate to cope with a major shift in consumption patterns to materials which are not readily biodegradable (over 40 per cent of Shengze residents claimed the composition of their rubbish had changed in recent years compared with around five per cent of respondents in each of the other two *zhen*). Wastewater plumbing was virtually non-existent in Neiguan and Yuantan, although in Shengze over 60 per cent of surveyed households were connected to sewerage. Tap water was available to 94 per cent of surveyed Shengze households: elsewhere many residents abstracted water from streams or wells. The increased pollution loads associated with industrialisation, however, will increasingly call into question the safety of such sources: even underground water sources are vulnerable to pollution. Electricity, however, was available to all surveyed households in each of the three *zhen*. Household ownership of televisions, such a major force in shaping perceptions and aspirations, was over 80 per cent in Neiguan, 90 per cent in Yuantan and 99 per cent in Shengze.

Tensions between environment and development, which had been the initial stimulus for our work, were evident in each of the three *zhen*. Although official statistics were unavailable - and may well have been inaccurate - significant amounts of agricultural land had transferred out of agriculture in recent years, particularly in Yuantan and Shengze, for industrial and infrastructural developments and for new housing. This has occurred despite official regulations and a high degree of awareness about land regulations among residents (around 95 per cent of our respondents claimed they knew of such regulations), and the threat of punitive action against transgressors. Agricultural land loss is of course an inevitable consequence of the pursuance of a policy of rural industrialisation. The more immediate problem is to minimise the loss of the best agricultural land and to apply regulations in a consistent way. Both are hampered by the priority accorded short-term economic imperatives, and the administration of building by two agencies, one dealing with land management and one dealing with urban construction. The lack of coordination between these agencies was frequently commented upon by staff and was clearly an impediment to more rational land-use. A similar situation applied to pollution. As with land, comprehensive regulations were in place to restrict emissions from industrial activities, but there was a mismatch between the official position and the situation on the ground. Implementation of environmental regulations has been particularly problematic in the countryside and has resulted in the transplantation of highly polluting industries from the urban centres where industrial activities are more easily policed. We were told that some enterprises coped with pollution regulations by meeting emission targets on the dates of inspection, or simply by paying any fines which were levied. A further problem we encountered was the acute shortage of personnel who were well trained in environmental protection work: we believe this to be another major obstacle to progress.

However, it would be misleading to portray the *zhen* leaders and residents as being indifferent to the question of environmental quality. Both were well aware of land and pollution issues. We found that in the most advanced *zhen* significantly fewer residents were prepared to accept additional polluting industries, even if it meant increased wealth for the town, than in the two less advanced *zhen*. It seems that a combination of increased wealth and a longer familiarity with the externalities of industrialisation have tempered enthusiasm for further such developments here. Significantly, in Neiguan and Yuantan it was the younger and better educated respondents who were most sensitive to environmental issues. Despite such optimistic signs the environmental problems associated with rural industrialisation and urbanisation - land loss and pollution in particular - will not easily be resolved. We remain committed to the view that failure to reconcile these issues will impact significantly on China's food production capacity and environmental quality in the 21st century.

Bibliography

Byrd, W. and Lin Qingsong (eds) (1990), *China's Rural Industry: Structure, Development and Reform*, Oxford University Press, Oxford.

Fei Hsiao-Tung (Fei Xiaotong) (1939), *Peasant Life in China: A Field Study of Country Life in the Yangtze Valley*, Routledge, London.

Fei Xiaotong (ed) (1986), *Small Towns in China: Functions, Problems and Prospects*, New World Press, Beijing.

Fei Xiaotong (1994), 'The Road to China's Urban and Rural Development: A Subject of My Lifetime's Research', *China City Planning Review*, March, pp. 2-11.

Kirkby, R.J.R. (1982), 'Settlement Policy for a Modernising China', in J. Taylor and D. Williams (eds), *Urban Planning Practice in Developing Countries*, Pergamon Press, Oxford, pp. 189-214.

Kirkby, R.J.R. (1985), *Urbanisation in China: Town and Country in a Developing Economy 1949-2000 AD*, Croom Helm, London.

Kirkby, R.J.R. (1988), 'The Environmental Constraints on China's Rural Urbanisation Strategy: An Essay of the Past, Present and Future', *Asian Geographer*, vol. 15, pp. 123-41.

Kirkby, R.J.R. (1994), 'Dilemmas of Urbanisation: Review and Prospects', in D. Dwyer (ed), *China: The Next Decades*, Longman, Harlow, pp. 156-85.

Lee, Y-S.F. (1989), 'Small Towns and China's Urbanization Level', *China Quarterly*, vol. 120, pp. 771-88.

Liu Guobin (1999), 'Soil Conservation and Sustainable Agriculture on the Loess Plateau', *Ambio*, vol. 28, pp. 663-8.

Luo Maochu (1988), 'A Review and Evaluation of China's Policy for the Development of Small Towns', *China City Planning Review*, vol. 4, pp. 22-37.

Ma, L.J.C. and Ming Fan (1994), 'Urbanisation From Below: The Growth of Small Towns in Jiangsu, China', *Urban Studies*, vol. 31, pp. 1625-45.

McGee, T. G. (1989), 'Urbanisasi or Kotadesasi? Evolving Patterns of Urbanization in Asia', in A. Costa *et al* (eds), *Urbanization in*

Asia: Spatial Dimensions and Policy Issues, University of Hawaii Press, Honolulu.

Ministry of Construction (1996), 'China: Report on the Development of Human Settlements', *China City Planning Review*, vol. 12, pp. 12-22.

Muldavin, J. (1998), 'The Limits to Market Triumphalism in Rural China', *Geoforum*, vol. 28, pp. 289-312.

National Environmental Protection Agency and State Planning Commission (1994), *Zhongguo Huanjing Baohu Xingdong Jihua 1991-2000 Nian* (*Action Plan for China's Environmental Protection, 1991-2000*), China Environmental Science Press, Beijing.

Qu Geping and Li Jinchang (1994), *Population and the Environment in China*, Lynne Rienner, Boulder.

State Statistical Bureau (1995), *Statistical Yearbook of China, 1995*, Statistical Information and Consultancy Service Centre, Beijing.

State Statistical Bureau (1996), *Statistical Yearbook of China 1996*, Statistical Information and Consultancy Service Centre, Beijing.

Tan, K.C. (1988), 'Regional Variation in the Growth Patterns of Chinese Small Towns', unpublished paper, *4th Asian Urbanization Conference*, Nanjing, August 1988.

Wei Houkai (1997), 'Economic Result of Urban Size and Location Planning Policies in China', Unpublished paper, *European Agricultural and Rural Development Conference*, Manchester, May 1997.

World Bank (1997), *China 2020*, The World Bank, Washington.

Zhang Jiacheng and Lin Zhiguang (1992), *Climate of China*, John Wiley and Sons, Chichester.

Zhao Songqiao (1986), *Physical Geography of China*, Science Press, Beijing/John Wiley and Sons, Chichester.

Zhao Xiaobin and Li Zhang (1995), 'Urban Performance and the Control of Urban Size in China', *Urban Studies*, vol. 32, pp. 813-42.

Zhou Yixing and Yu Ting (1989), 'Discussion of China's Urban Development Policy', *Chinese Geography and the Environment*, Summer 1989, pp. 76-86.

Index

151